MY WOUNDED HEART

A PASTOR'S STORY

*Responding Positively to Hurt in
Order to Return to Wholeness*

I've had the privilege of knowing Benny Woods for over twenty years. He is a man who has a heart for God. His compassion for pastors was born in the fire of conflict in a local church. I understand that because, I, too, have felt the same pain of rejection. God has uniquely called Benny and Carolyn to reach out to the multitude of pastors who have been deeply wounded in the ministry. Benny not only survived his wounds, but God used them as the seeds to call him to touch many lives.

Chuck McAlister former Pastor
Second Baptist Church
Hot Springs, Arkansas

In looking over your website, I want to say I am grateful that you've undertaken this endeavor and are doing so in a great way. The needs are overwhelming and I again am grateful you've chosen to minister to those who minister. The website is appealing and contains good information. Working with pastors and ministry staff to encourage and restore their ministries is a worthy calling. I'm encouraged that you've respond to the call.

Roy Blankenship, Minister of Communication and Counseling
First Baptist Church, Woodstock, Georgia

I had the privilege of meeting Benny Woods just a few years ago. In my brief encounters with him, I found him to be a man with a heart for God and a love for Christ and people. Certainly, no one would attempt such a demanding ministry as Benny is thinking of without the Holy Spirit's leadership. It takes a man of compassion and stability to consider such an outreach. My sense is that Benny and Carolyn have that capability.

Jim Henry, former Pastor
First Baptist Church of Orlando, Florida
Former President of the Southern Baptist Convention

God bless you and your ministry in every way. This is such a needed ministry and all of us need to work together to provide everything possible.

In His love, James T. Draper, Jr.
Former President, Lifeway Christian Resources

MY WOUNDED HEART

A PASTOR'S STORY

*Responding Positively to Hurt in
Order to Return to Wholeness*

BENNY WOODS

WESTBOW
PRESS®
A DIVISION OF THOMAS NELSON
& ZONDERVAN

Scripture quotations taken from the New American Standard Bible®, Copyright © 1960, 1962, 1963, 1968, 1971, 1972, 1973, 1975, 1977, 1995 by The Lockman Foundation. Used by permission. (www.Lockman.org)

WestBow Press books may be ordered through booksellers or by contacting:

WestBow Press
A Division of Thomas Nelson & Zondervan
1663 Liberty Drive
Bloomington, IN 47403
www.westbowpress.com
1 (866) 928-1240

Because of the dynamic nature of the Internet, any web addresses or links contained in this book may have changed since publication and may no longer be valid. The views expressed in this work are solely those of the author and do not necessarily reflect the views of the publisher, and the publisher hereby disclaims any responsibility for them.

Any people depicted in stock imagery provided by Thinkstock are models, and such images are being used for illustrative purposes only. Certain stock imagery © Thinkstock.

ISBN: 978-1-5127-1134-9 (sc)
ISBN: 978-1-5127-1135-6 (hc)
ISBN: 978-1-5127-1133-2 (e)

Library of Congress Control Number: 2015914586

Print information available on the last page.

WestBow Press rev. date: 09/21/2015

DEDICATION

To Carolyn, my best friend and life partner, the one to whom I owe a tremendous debt of gratitude for her unselfish loyalty, support, and unwavering faithfulness over a span of half a century; and to our daughter, Carrie, whose life is the greatest compliment to our lives and ministry.

CONTENTS

FOREWORD.

My Wounded Heart is a compelling book that describes a pastor's painful experience of hurt and rejection and how God brought him and his family through this experience. It also describes the process of emotional healing and restoration, by God's grace, to the point where Pastor Benny and his wife are now being used by God to minister to others who have been through, or are going through, traumatic experiences. The book gives practical, biblical principles and guidance for those who are wounded and seeking God's healing.

The treatment of physical wounds and reconstruction form a major component of my practice as a plastic surgeon. Wounds can heal with time, but healed wounds always leave scars, reminding the person of the wound. Deep, extensive, or infected wounds may not heal on their own and often require surgical removal of damaged skin and tissue. Reconstructive surgery can be done, bringing in new tissue or skin, resulting in a modified or renewed appearance. Yet, even with the best surgery, a faint scar will be detectable. Scientific research is yet to find a way to achieve complete wound healing or tissue regeneration without leaving a scar. God in His infinite wisdom designed the human body in this way for a reason.

Similarly, healed emotional wounds also leave scars, as Pastor Benny shows in his book. Often in life, the past gets in the way of the future. Deep emotional scars can be difficult to deal with. However, unless the root cause is dealt with or removed, true progress cannot be made.

Having personally seen the work of Pastor Benny at the Bangalore Baptist Hospital, I know him to be a man of impeccable character, commanding warm affection and respect from his colleagues and the patients he serves. The chaplaincy service at the hospital is a busy department, ministering to church leaders, students, and patients who are going through intense pain and suffering. Pastor Benny brings with him his rich experience in dealing with pain and suffering in difficult circumstances, with a complete foundation on the Bible and the Word of God.

"The LORD is close to the brokenhearted and saves those who are crushed in spirit" (Psalm 34:18).

I sincerely hope that this book challenges you, as it has done for me. More importantly, it seeks to encourage those persons who are going through a similar experience in their lives.

I admire Pastor Benny and Carolyn for their amazing faith journey and thank them for their efforts in helping others through their personal testimony. I speak on behalf of all the patients at the Bangalore Baptist Hospital in reminding them that they are a great source of blessing, support and *hope*.

Dr. Derick Mendonca, FRCS (Plastic)
Consultant Plastic Surgeon
Bangalore Baptist Hospital
Bangalore, India

PREFACE

Christmas has always been such a special time for our family. We have a large collection of Christmas ornaments that have been collected over a number of years. On each trip or vacation, we always bought a Christmas ornament. There are the special ones made by small hands while our daughter was in kindergarten. There are those that were given to us by our dear friends. Each year as the three of us decorate the tree, we talk about the ornaments and share the memories that go with them.

The last ornament to be placed on the tree is the topper that we purchased for our very first tree. It is an inexpensive glass topper bought at a discount store in Fort Bragg, North Carolina, during Benny's military days. This ornament is very special to us. Once the tree was decorated, the topper placed on top. Then came the photograph of the decorated tree for that year.

The year 1996 was to be a different sort of Christmas. Our daughter, Carrie, was away at college in Alabama. The church where we served was in turmoil. My husband did not want to put up the tree, so I did it myself. With the holiday drawing closer, I did the things we always had done in preparing for Christmas.

One day when I returned from shopping, I walked into our living room to find my husband—the strong man he was, my pastor and spiritual leader—lying on the floor beside the Christmas tree, deeply emotionally upset and crying.

What had brought us to this point in our lives and ministry? For the rest of the story, keep reading . . .

Carolyn Woods
Nashville, Tennessee
April 21, 2014

ACKNOWLEDGMENTS

The writing of this book has been a work in progress, involving both my heart and mind, over a period of many years. It is a book born out of the furnace of pain and the ashes of rejection. Other sufferers like my wife and me have made countless contributions to the writing of this book. During numerous counseling sessions by phone and via the Internet and face-to-face encounters with the hurting and wounded, my life has taken the shape of a wounded healer as I have entered into their worlds with them. Therefore, the book is not only about me and my wounded heart, which is a mere microcosm in light of the many who have gone through the fires of pain and rejection (and many of whom, by the grace of a loving heavenly Father, have found healing, forgiveness, and restoration).

I am grateful to my wife Carolyn, my partner in ministry for 40 years and life partner for 51 years. She has stood by my side through thick and thin to encourage me. Together we have trudged down memory lane in recalling events, circumstances, and situations in the writing of this book, many of which were painful and hurtful experiences. But we are thankful that the good experiences have outweighed the bad.

Then there is Basil Frasure, PhD, founder of Whole Person Counseling, who granted me permission to use his invaluable counseling materials in Section II of my book, and to whom I am grateful.

My editor, Mr. Sahu, did some initial editing, which has been invaluable as well. His input early on was very helpful. Many other contributions have been made by noted authors whose quotes appear throughout the book, and to whom I am also grateful.

I reserve this final word for my publisher, WestBow Publishing that took up my project in midstream and led this new author through the twists and turns of writing to the books final completion. I will always be grateful for their faithful and helpful assistance.

Benny Woods
Nashville, Tennessee
April 2014

PROLOGUE

The panorama of the beautiful grasslands of the vast expanse seen from our northwestern home with its sliding glass doors, was breathtaking for my wife, Carolyn, and me. Our home was located in a beautiful section of the Northwest. Having lived in the Midwest, we had been accustomed to the vastness of the open countryside. From our back deck, which extended the length of our house, we could see the beautiful mountain range high above the pasturelands. The vastness of the open range complemented the ascending mountain range seen in the distance.

From our perspective, we could see to the west the dark clouds in the distance, moving in our direction, with lightning flashing and the sound of thunder. We did not need the weatherman to tell us that a storm was brewing on the horizon. Being many miles away, we had time to prepare as we enjoyed the sights and sounds of the forces of nature.

Like the storms of nature, the storms of life come—but one is rarely prepared for the devastation and trauma left in their wake.

In 1997, Carolyn and I faced a storm of life for which we were not prepared. Although our storm paled in comparison with what others have experienced, it rent our hearts and made flotsam of our emotions. It was a time when we were blindsided by the worst we could ever imagine. It seemed we were constantly either in a storm or coming out of one and getting ready for another.

Unlike the storm we could see through our sliding glass doors as it gathered over our home and spread its cloak over the valley below, little did we know at that time that our life-storm was forming.

Now, many years later, we have survived the storm, been rescued, fully recovered, and experienced restoration after the storm; thus, the content of this book begs to be read by anyone getting ready to go through a storm, presently in a storm, or coming out of a storm.

Since storms of life often wound a person emotionally and leave them with a wounded heart, as was true in this writer's case, help is often needed while in the storm—but especially while recovering from the storm.

That is what this book is about: a wounded heart . . . and how to not only survive the storm, but also fully recover from the storm.

Section I of this book contains this writer's personal story of life at its best and how life's storms can invade a life at any time and anywhere, leaving an individual with a wounded heart.

Section II, however, offers practical, biblically-based counseling—Whole Person Counseling (Frasure) if you please, which involves the whole person, i.e. body, soul, and spirit.

A disclaimer . . .

In no way is this book written to vindicate emotional wounds suffered at the hands of others, mar the reputation of another person, or cast the writer in a better light. While names and places are fictional to protect the identity of persons involved, the story is true to the best of this writer's recollection and personal diary.

Of course, certain of the writer's biases are unavoidable. If persons involved in this writer's story wrote from their own perspective, their biases would, perhaps, emerge as well. That being said, however, this book is about healing and recovery for persons who have been wounded emotionally.

Consider the case of Joseph in the Old Testament (Genesis 37—50), in which Joseph said to his brothers who had hurt him, "You meant evil against me, but God meant it for good…" (Genesis

50:20). As Joseph forgave his brothers, there is no unforgiveness, or bitterness, in this writer's heart toward anyone. The wounds have healed, and God has brought nothing but good out of a hurtful situation.

SECTION I

CHAPTER ONE

PULLING UP OUR ROOTS

It was on December 31, 1965, that I received an honorable discharge from the US Army, having served on active duty for three years. Now it was time to begin a new career. At the age of 21, I sought employment so that I could provide for my family. For a brief time I worked at a mortuary, until I found more permanent employment. Through the help of a dear friend and former employer, I landed a good job at a well-known chemical plant where I would work for a period of almost nine years.

During those ensuing years, my wife and I became very active in our local Baptist church, under the leadership of a loving pastor who always challenged us to grow in our faith. Becoming more and more involved in the work of ministry, I became dissatisfied with my secular job and began sensing that God had a different plan and purpose for my life. After a four-year period of wrestling with the feelings that would not go away, believing that a call to ministry was a call to prepare, I enrolled in night school classes at a local extension of East Tennessee State University.

Now well into my studies at the university, and continuing to work at my secular job, I took a leap of faith during a Sunday morning worship service at our church and responded to God's call to full-time ministry.

Shortly after making my public commitment to God's call upon my life, I was licensed to preach by my church, and within days I was contacted by the pastor of our hometown church to preach in his absence on a Sunday morning. That preaching opportunity opened up the door to preach for him the next Sunday. Following that Sunday morning of preaching, Carolyn and I went out for lunch at a local restaurant and learned from some of the church members that the pastor had resigned.

Within days, I was contacted by church leaders inviting me to return to preach again now that they were without a pastor. It was not long thereafter that I was invited to become the interim pastor by the church's leadership. This interim made it possible for me to resign my secular job and continue my college education full-time.

Becoming the interim pastor of my hometown church became a rich experience and reaffirmed my call to the ministry. The church took this young, unpolished speaker, a semi-educated man without pastoral experience, under their wings, loving and accepting him and his family unconditionally. The feeling was indeed mutual. We loved them as well.

Shortly after I became the interim pastor, the church requested that I be ordained in order for me to perform my many duties as their interim. At their request, I was duly ordained on March 23, 1974.

I will always be grateful to the first church where I served as interim pastor for giving this pastor his start in serving a church.

While I served as interim in my hometown, a search committee came by one Sunday morning to hear me speak. After the service we met, and they invited me to come to their church for a trial sermon. Negotiations continued over the ensuing days. I preached a trial sermon some time later, and the church ultimately extended to me a call to be their pastor, which I accepted. Upon our departure from my interim position in our hometown, the church gave us a tremendous send-off. We still cherish the sterling silver serving set the church gave us as a going-away gift.

It was agreed during negotiations prior to my becoming the pastor of a church located in another part of East Tennessee that I could continue my college education. After moving onto the church field in January of 1976, I transferred from my former university to the University of Tennessee, Knoxville. This was in my senior year.

The church I was now serving was located in a small town, in the plains connected to the beautiful Cherokee National Forest, in the foothills of the Great Smoky Mountains. The river running through the forest afforded this outdoorsman some relaxing trout fishing in between classes at the university and my ministry to the church.

These mountain folk adopted the Woods family into their loving care, and our relationship as pastor and people grew over the forthcoming months.

At long last, graduation time came, and I received my Bachelor of Arts degree from the university. For about six months, I was content to be out of school and gave my full focus to the church. The time came, however, when I began considering going on to seminary.

While I was praying in my study early one morning, my phone rang. On the phone was a seasoned pastor, denominational leader, mentor, and trusted friend. He said, "Benny, I think you ought to go to seminary!" That was the answer to my prayer. But how would I approach the church on this matter since they had already allowed me to finish my college work? To complicate matters, the seminary closest to our home was located some three hundred miles to the north. I talked it over with Carolyn, and we decided to move forward with asking the church for permission to attend seminary. After much discussion when the question was placed before them, they granted me permission to attend seminary—one semester at a time.

Off I went on another educational adventure (Tuesday–Friday) while Carolyn performed the role of assistant pastor (our designation) during my absence. This was a difficult time for all of us with my being away from church and family four days a week and commuting over six hundred miles round trip.

After completing one year of seminary, the time came for us to make a decision. We both agreed that I should continue my seminary education. Once again I took my proposal to the church, and this time they said they needed a full-time pastor and that I must put my education on hold and stay with them full-time. Believing that God had spoken and I must continue my education, I resigned. The church gave us our two-week vacation pay and a great send off, and we loaded the U-Haul truck and were on our way to seminary.

Carolyn and my nine-year-old daughter had grown to love the church people and the beautiful Cherokee National Forest, and as it had been in the past, we found that leaving folks and places you love is no easy matter. Nevertheless, we said our good-byes and were on our way.

Arriving on campus, with no job in sight, I became very frightened for my family and myself. It was not long, however, before we got a position with a children's home located near the seminary I would be attending. We were responsible for 12 troubled teenage girls. Carolyn was the houseparent and I was her assistant. This freed me up to be a full-time seminary student. We were privileged to serve in that position for six months until a church within a two-hour drive of the seminary called me to be their pastor. They allowed me to commute back and forth to seminary while serving as pastor.

As at the two previous churches, we developed a beautiful love relationship with the new church families and with the girls at the children's home.

The church we were privileged to serve was in a farm community consisting primarily of burley tobacco and dairy farms. Because I came from a farm background myself, I was on common ground with the farmers and their families. They loved us, and we loved them.

On a fall Sunday morning, a search committee from a Midwestern state visited the church where I was pastor to hear me preach. Apparently they liked what they heard and invited me to come to their church for a trial sermon. If this opportunity materialized, this would be my first church free of the exception of one semester of Hebrew, which I wo complete before I could graduate. If called to be their pasto have to commute for three months.

After some long delays and revisiting the negotiation ta the Midwestern church search committee extended a call to me to become their pastor. Once again, we said our good-byes to the good folks at the church, whom we had grown to love during the past year. They, like the previous churches we served, were saddened as we were to separate from them, but they gave us a wonderful send-off.

In retrospect of our resigning and leaving our seminary pastorate, our journey had taken us from the hills of the Southeast to the beautiful farmlands of the Northeast, and then on to the flatlands of the Midwest, landscaped by the unending fields of corn and soybeans surrounding the small city where we would be serving.

The unselfish giving of both Carolyn and Carrie made it possible for me to earn two education degrees—college and seminary—by the time I was called to be pastor of our new church.

During our ministry journey to this point, I had gained a lot of pastoral experience. Now, ready or not, the challenge was before me to pastor a church in the Midwest. The uprooting process continued. I graduated from seminary in 1981, and we moved to the Midwest, where my family and I had the privilege of serving a wonderful church for more than a decade.

We had accepted a pastorate in which the congregation had been deeply wounded as a result of internal conflict, and finding the church, as it were, lying on its back kicking, the challenge was before us as a young pastor, wife, and daughter. The time for healing was at hand for this wounded congregation. Emotions were still tender and in need of healing upon our arrival.

Prior to our accepting the church's call, the church had gone through a literal split; leaving two fragmented groups of believers.

In retrospect of answering the church's call, it took me some time to sort out what had happened to cause the division before

ide the ministry that would bring healing
onflict had left the church suffering from
d in need of healing.

indeed, caused a storm in the body of
inning to recover from the storm when
e storm, the members were in desperate
ve since learned, having had Clinical
... (CPE), this body of believers needed healing,
...onciling, nurturing, sustaining, and guiding, in keeping with
the five traditions of pastoral care as exemplified in the life and
ministry of Jesus.

I was the young pastor God had called to this ministry
assignment. All five traditions of pastoral care would be needed to
bring this church to recovery and full restoration. Unbeknownst to
us at the time, God, in His infinite wisdom, was allowing us to meet
this church coming out of the storm in order to prepare us for the
storm that would eventually invade our lives.

The anointing oil of reconciliation and forgiveness would be
the first step in bringing healing to this wounded body of believers.
Almost immediately, I began a series of sermons from the Old
Testament book of Nehemiah titled A New Beginning. Bathed in
prayer, this sermon series was the first step in starting the healing
process, in bringing restoration and healing to this wounded body.
After healing and reconciliation, nurturing, guiding, and sustaining
would ultimately follow in no particular order. Thus, over a period
of many months, new life began to emerge among the members.
Although scars from previous hurts remained, it was obvious that
reconciliation had occurred, guidance had been given, and the
church was now in the sustaining mode.

As a result, over a period of time, the church slowly began to
grow numerically, recover emotionally, develop spiritually, and be
recognized among the sister churches as a growing and progressive
church. Baptisms, buildings, and budgets became the order of the
day, as in the book of Nehemiah, "for the people had a mind to

work" (Nehemiah 4:6), a heart to forgive, and a desire to recover from their wounds.

Restoration had come to this church, which began as a mission in the heartland of the Midwest many years earlier. After ten and one-half years on the church field, and having witnessed the church's restoration under the leadership of the Holy Spirit, I sensed that God was calling me to a new assignment.

The first indication of a move came quite unexpectedly. Call it women's intuition if you will, but Carolyn received a late Christmas card in January from the wife of a former deacon, who had left the church we were serving in the Midwest to be assigned to an Air Force base in another state. After receiving the card in January of 1990, Carolyn said to me, "Benny, we are going to be moving soon!"

Following these words, in early January of 1991, I received a call from a member of a search committee in the Northwest, asking me to consider becoming their pastor. If the possibility of a move materialized, it would be a tough decision since we were in the appointment process with a foreign mission board. We had been invited to consider becoming foreign missionaries. This process had begun at the request of an employee of the board. Having agreed to begin the appointment process, we were assigned to a consultant on the board who would lead us through the appointment process.

It had become quite apparent to us at this time that God was rearranging our circumstances and that, ultimately, we would have to make a big decision. Wherever God's Spirit led us, the move would not be easy.

The move would be softened, however, by the fact that our daughter, Carrie, had completed her high school education and was now enrolled as a freshman at a university in the Southeast. She had said to me upon our arrival at our new church, "Daddy, can we stay here until I graduate high school?" Certainly, I could not make her any promises regarding that request, but it would become a reality, and by that time she would have moved on to another phase of her life. Sending her off to college many miles away had not been easy for her mother and I, nor was being disconnected from her church family and special friends easy for Carrie, especially now that we were leaving.

Leaving our pastorate and the church family in the Midwest would be even more difficult for Carolyn. This had become her home. She did not want to leave. In her own words, in regard to a possible move, she said, "I could have stayed here forever." I, too, would miss the vast countryside just a few minutes outside of town, where the city gave way to the seemingly never-ending corn and soybean fields.

Having grown up on a farm in East Tennessee, I had thoroughly enjoyed life in the farmland of mid-America. I cannot recount the numerous hours I spent in prayer with the Father while driving through the countryside, surrounded by soybean and cornfields and gazing across the beautiful farmland. The early morning sunrise was especially beautiful, and as an avid biker, I would often pause for a brief moment while on my way to the church to behold God's beautiful creation. I would gaze at the sunrise and drink to the full, in the words of the prophet Isaiah, that "the whole earth is full of His glory" (Isaiah 6:3).

In the Midwest, we were privileged to serve a people many of whom had migrated from the South to find jobs at two major factories and the steel mill. Because of this connection with the southern members and all the wonderful people we had grown to love, made our leaving more difficult.

The financial security we enjoyed and the delight in serving a healthy church that had risen from the dust and ashes of division would not soon be forgotten. Nevertheless, we had to obey the call of God.

As anticipated, the call to pastor the northwestern church did come, and we accepted. Our date for arrival on the church field would be October 29, 1991. We would be leaving the vast farmland of mid-America to live in the Northwest.

The sendoff the church gave us as we prepared to move left little to be desired. Gifts were given, loving hugs were exchanged, and many tears were shed. This separation of pastor and people was laced with mixed emotions; both tears of joy and sadness were shed at the time of our separation. In light of our emotional sendoff, I remembered so vividly the Sunday morning the church had celebrated our tenth anniversary as their pastor. It was during that celebration that the church gave us a paid vacation to the Ozarks to see a Passion play.

I remember also the Sunday morning I met with the deacons to let them know that I would be going to a church in the Northwest to meet with a search committee in view of a call. When I made that announcement, my dear deacon friend and chairman of deacons began to weep at the thought of his pastor leaving. This was the same deacon and wonderful friend, a man big in stature, which had put his strong arms around me and comforted me upon learning of my father's sudden death. While working on a building project at the church on a Saturday morning, I had received a call from my brother that Daddy had died of a heart attack. My friend was the first one on the scene to embrace me. I shall never forget that moment.

Back to the meeting . . . I must admit that all of us who were present at that meeting were moved emotionally. What none of us knew at the time was that, after the move to the Northwest, I would return to conduct the funeral of our long-time friend. He died of cancer shortly after we moved. I share this as a way of describing the kind of relationship we had with our wonderful church family. This is why moving was so difficult. In previous moves, I had never shared with the deacons beforehand that a possible move was in my future. Normally, I did not make the announcement that I was leaving until I had been called by a church. Having such a close relationship, I did not want to surprise them about moving after the fact. As this was such an important move, I wanted the deacons to pray for us not only about the church, but also the mission appointment process, in which we were engaged as well.

These are just a few more highlights of our eventful separations from people and churches we had grown to love.

Following the confirmation of the call, we put our house up for sale. I gave the church a one-month notice of separation, in keeping with the church's policy. Then, one month later, after a meaningful Sunday evening of worship and a time of tearful good-byes, we left on the following Monday morning for our new place of ministry.

CHAPTER TWO

ON THE ROAD AGAIN

In retrospect of our move to a northwestern state, the process unfolded while on the trip the church had given us to the aforementioned Passion play. Shortly after our ten-year celebration as pastor of the Midwest church, we used that time to negotiate with the search committee of the Northwest church about a possible move. The process unfolded as plans were made with the search committee. It would be after these conversations that we agreed to return for a second visit with the search committee.

Arrangements were made with a sister church for me to preach for the pastor search committee. I would arrive at the designated church on Sunday morning and meet with the pastor of the church. I would then be introduced to the church by a member of the search committee and deliver the message. It was so nice of the young pastor to surrender his pulpit to me in order to preach a message for the search committee.

Following what I believe to be one of the worst sermons I had delivered up to that time, the search committee met and made a decision whether or not to invite me back for a trial sermon. Invite me they did. To be honest, I was surprised that they extended a call to me. I remember one of the committee members saying to me later that day as we travelled from the church and discussed the morning message, "We were so desperate for a pastor we would have called you even if you had fallen out of the pulpit." Laughingly, I said, "I don't think I can take that as a compliment." Be that as it may, the search committee extended an invitation to return in view of a call.

It was on our return trip to the Northwest, in view of a call and following our vacation to the Ozarks (and after having shared with the deacons that we might be moving) that we had to begin thinking seriously about finding a new home.

Finding and purchasing our new home is an interesting story. It was on our second visit to the city where I would be serving as pastor, and the weekend during which I preached the trial sermon, that we tentatively purchased a house.

Time was of the essence to find a home, considering the probability of being called as pastor. This meant that it was important for us to find a place to live on the Saturday before our return home. If we did not find a house on this visit, and if the church did call us, we would have to make a third trip back to find a place to live. Always in the past, as we moved to a new church field, we found the right house—the one that God had for us. We were anticipating a similar experience this time.

Arising early on Saturday morning to attend a meeting at the church and then begin our search for a house caused no little stress—especially for Carolyn. The realtor we hired had taken us to view a lot of houses, but nothing to this point seemed quite suitable.

Before leaving the hotel, as time was running out for us to find a house, Carolyn became quite upset and was crying. Consoling and encouraging her as best I could, I walked over to the window overlooking the city and prayed, "Lord, for Carolyn's sake, we need to find a house today!" The emphasis was on "today"!

Once we got dressed and attended the church meeting, we had only the afternoon to find a place to live. Quickly, we got into the car and headed out on a house search. We drove south after we took the first right and then a sharp turn in the road, Carolyn spotted a sign in the front yard of a little brown house that read, "Home for

Sale!" As I drove past the sign, Carolyn yelled out, "Benny, stop! Did you see that sign? Back up!"

I immediately stopped, put the car in reverse, and then pulled into the driveway. We got out of the car, walked up to the front door, knocked, and were greeted by an elderly couple that was very friendly. We introduced ourselves and immediately asked, "Could we look at your house?"

"Sure!" they answered. "Come on in!" As we moved out of the foyer and entered the house, the kitchen was the first room we observed. Carolyn loved the kitchen. Then we moved from the kitchen to the living room. We were amazed at what we saw. The living room gave way to an amazing view through the sliding glass doors. The view could be described in European terms as "Belvedere—a house with a view."

To our amazement, from the living room and through the sliding glass doors leading out to the deck, we had nothing less than a panoramic view of the beautiful pasturelands, with the mountains towering in the background. The view was uninhabited by people, and the grasslands were dotted with cows grazing in the distance.

Although the lovely couple escorted us through the remaining part of the house, our minds were already made up. If possible, this would become our new home. As had happened in the past when relocating and looking for a new home, everything about this place said, *This is it.*

Almost immediately, negotiations began with the owners. After some legal action and waiting to finalize the deal, and, of course, following the church vote, this beautiful "Home for Sale" would become ours.

The Sunday we had been waiting for finally came, and I found myself in the prospective church, preaching the trial sermon. Standing behind the pulpit, I opened my Bible to Jeremiah 18:1–12 and spoke on the subject "The Potter and the Clay." I preached at both services, and the church voted on Sunday night following the service. Prior to the church being called to order for the vote,

Carolyn and I were escorted to an adjacent office to wait until the votes were cast.

The wait was very short. The door flung open, and a tall Air Force officer who was stationed at a nearby Air Force base, and who also served as a deacon and member of the search committee, said, "Welcome, Pastor! You have just been called to be our pastor." He immediately escorted us back to the sanctuary, where the waiting members applauded as we entered. We were led to the front of the podium, where the members came by to welcome us as their new pastor and wife. Carolyn and I responded with hugs and loving handshakes. This was the perfect ending to what had been a great day.

Before leaving our Midwest home, and after having been called to pastor the northwestern state, we left our home in the hands of a realtor and began making plans to move.

On moving day, we watched the moving company load our belongings on the moving van. It had been a week since we had said our final good-byes to our wonderful church family. It was now Monday morning. Once the truck was loaded, in the words of Willie Nelson, we were "on the road again."[1]

I was driving our family car, leading the way, and Carolyn and Mr. Sam were following in his Buick. We had adopted this elderly gentleman, now in his late eighties, following his wife's death a few years earlier.

In explanation . . . During our time in the Midwest, this couple had unofficially adopted the Woods family, and we had become very close to them. While I visited with the wife in the hospital just a few hours before her death, she had asked me to promise to take care of her husband when she died. So, upon her death, we took Mr. Sam into our home, and he became a part of our family.

Our trip across the country to our new home and church would be a two-day drive, since we did not want our travelling companion to be worn out, physically, from the long drive. Our furniture had been loaded onto the moving truck and would be unloaded at our new home upon our arrival. I will always remember moving day.

We could hardly wait to get moved into our new dream home. For now, however, we were enjoying the journey. Driving by myself, with Carolyn and Mr. Sam following close behind, I had time to spend quiet moments meditating and talking to the Father and enjoying the beautiful drive. Stopping occasionally to stretch our legs and take bathroom breaks, we felt the excitement build as we drove cross-country.

Once we reached the state line and passed through a well-known city en route to our final destination, the last leg of our journey was upon us, and it was a long one at that. Immediately after crossing into our designated state, we passed the time by reading the many billboards. These road signs kept reappearing all along the way as the mile listing decreased. We thought about what we would find when we arrived at our final destination. The drive itself was turning out to be quite an adventure. The drive thus far had been very enjoyable, but would get even better now that we had crossed the state line and moved into the wide-open spaces.

The drive for me, a hunter and lover of the great outdoors, became even more interesting. My eyes were like binoculars looking for wildlife and enjoying the open spaces of the Northwest Territory. Occasionally I would spot a ring-necked pheasant along the side of the road and make an attempt to get Carolyn's attention by pointing in the direction of the pheasant and looking in my rearview mirror to see if perhaps she had spotted it.

Along the way, tumbleweed would occasionally roll across the road in front of me, pushed along by the wind, and I would watch it disappear along the roadside as I passed on by. These moving objects seemed to be alive. The most amazing sight was the evening sunset. It seemed to linger forever before cascading beneath the horizon. This amazing sunset elicited another prayer session for me.

As I prayed with enthusiasm and excitement at the thought of arriving at our destination and beginning our ministry at our new church, I asked the Father, "Do You have a word for me as I enter the city where I will be pastor?" In my mind, He spoke to me, and I heard Him as if He was speaking audibly. His answer was, "Take the city for Christ!" Somewhat overwhelmed by what I thought I heard Him saying to me, I determined in my mind to be obedient to His call to the best of my ability.

Those words became my marching orders for the next five and one-half years. God had given me a vision for a city whose population numbered more than fifty thousand. It was a tourist town as well, and would be inhabited by many visitors during the summer—many of whom would stop to worship with us on any given Sunday.

In the early nineties, a car phone was a luxury, and who would have believed the handheld cell phone would revolutionize our communication as it has today? I had a car phone that had been sold to me by a church member who owned a phone company. He gave me a special deal on the phone, and so I became the proud pastor of a car phone. The car phone allowed me the privilege of calling ahead and speaking with one of the ministry staff, whom we had met on a previous visit and who reassured me that there was a city at the end of our drive. During our brief conversation, he said to me, "Just keep on driving; you are almost here." The final leg of the journey gave me ample time to retrace the steps that had ultimately brought us to our new ministry.

Finally, the end was in sight. In the distance, about fifty miles away, I could see the light from the city piercing the darkness. It was late evening now, and the sun had finally disappeared behind the horizon. We were getting close to our destination. As I had guessed, the road sign read 50 Miles. It would take us about another hour to arrive at our new home and church.

Upon our arrival at the church, staff and other members we had met on our initial visits greeted us. There was a lot of excitement among those persons greeting their new pastor and wife, and we were excited as well, though tired from our long journey. Not too tired, however, to be given a second tour of the church facility before being taken to our hotel for the night. Carolyn and I both recalled later that as we toured the facility, especially the sanctuary, we had some really negative feelings, as if there were an evil presence. Passing it off as fatigue from the long journey, and because we were somewhat disoriented, we moved on with the exciting tour of the facilities. That evil presence we sensed was to be experienced again at a future time.

For now, caught up in the excitement of it all, we moved on from the sanctuary to the pastor's study. In retrospect of our first exposure to the church facility, I passed by what seemed to be a perfect room for an office or study, but which was being used as a storage room. In passing, I alluded to the fact that it would make a beautiful pastor's study. Well, to my surprise, someone had heard my desire, and—in the time between our two trips—this storage room had been converted into a beautiful pastor's study. It was equipped with a fireplace, new carpet had been laid, and a new desk and chair had been purchased. The most beautiful part of all was an adjacent prayer room. I was thrilled that someone had heard my desire for that space to be used as my office/study, and surprised that it was now mine.

This would become my meeting place with the Father for the next five years; it was where I prayed, prepared sermons, and counseled members—and from my window perspective, I watched the changing seasons, enjoying fully my beautiful surroundings. Occasionally I would spot deer, and some wild turkeys came almost close enough to reach out and touch. The hunter in me visualized the time when I could be out there in the wild with rifle in hand, looking for that prize buck. These were the early beginnings of an exciting time of ministry and life in the open spaces of the Northwest.

Our arrival at the church occurred late on a Friday evening, and following the tour of the church facility, we were escorted to our downtown hotel for our night's lodging. Following a good night of rest, we arose early the next morning and were greeted by the movers at our new place of residence. The truck with all our belongings had arrived safely.

The two-day trip to our new home and place of service was an interesting one indeed. Now, upon our arrival at our destination, the first task at hand was to unload, unpack, and get our possessions in place in our new home. We got out of bed early Saturday morning and drove from our hotel to our new home. Excitement continued to build as we anticipated moving.

This was such a beautiful day as we watched the movers offload our furniture and other possessions from the truck. As we stood outside watching the unfolding of events, with Mr. Sam seated comfortably near the garage and watching all the activity, a rancher and his cowhands drove a herd of cattle down the road just in front of our house. It reminded me of the many westerns I had seen on television and occasionally on the big screen over the years.

Here we were, right in the midst of the Northwest-watching cowboys, as it were, moving their herds. What a sight to behold! How excited we were to be in the open country of the Northwest, in our new home and beginning our new ministry. All in all, it was a great beginning for a new ministry as we unpacked and settled into our new place.

After a good night of rest back in our own beds, I do not know when I have been more excited about our first Sunday in a new church. I could hardly wait to get to the church, greet our new church family, and deliver my first message.

One could sense the excitement in the air upon our arrival that morning. The congregation was so excited to welcome their new pastor and first lady. As the morning worship service began, the choir did a wonderful job, the congregation sang with excitement and enthusiasm, and the atmosphere for worship was set for a message from God's Word.

After the special music by the church choir, I opened my Bible and delivered my first official sermon as the church's new pastor. I do not remember a time when I spoke with such power and enthusiasm. Bringing the message to a close, I gave the invitation, and two persons came forward to receive the gift of eternal life. What a day of rejoicing it had turned out to be on our first Sunday at our new church!

CHAPTER THREE

STORM WARNINGS

The area of the Northwest where we were now living is not known for predictability where winter storms are concerned. It has been said, and this certainly applies here, "If you don't like the weather, just wait—it will change." Change it did! After a wonderful day of worship, including the evening worship service, we came out of the worship center to find that the weather had changed from balmy, hours earlier, to a blast of winter.

Sleet was falling on this particular Sunday evening. This, of course, was the last Sunday in October, and anything could be expected where the weather was concerned. In fact, during the winter season, the Department of Transportation advises travelers to always have a safety survival kit in their vehicle. Winter advisories are fairly accurate, but blizzards or snowstorms can suddenly appear without warning. This is especially true of blowing snow that causes whiteouts on the highways—especially on the interstate.

On this October night, following the evening worship service, one could hear the sound of ice scrapers across the parking lot as church members were removing the ice from their car windshields. After removing the ice, all of us, including the other church members, made it safely home, but not with much time to spare since the storm front was becoming more pronounced moment by moment.

What happened on this Sunday evening would become a normal occurrence as we became more accustomed to the inclement weather of the Northwest. On one occasion, I remember a 100-degree change in the weather during a 24-hour period. I was playing golf with friends on a weekday afternoon, and the temperature was a warm 70 degrees. Twenty-four hours later, the temperature had fallen to 30 degrees below zero. Talk about change in the weather!

On Monday, we awoke to a full-blown blizzard and dared not leave our home as most of the roads were closed. The good news is that we had an ample supply of firewood stored in the garage, left by the previous owner. This allowed us to start a fire in our beautiful stone fireplace. So we settled in for the day, snuggled close to the fire, and enjoyed a cup of hot chocolate while anticipating a wonderful ministry at our new church and enjoying each other's company.

On Tuesday, the road crews were out clearing the roadways of snow banks and allowing the traffic to move about freely. The Department of Transportation was well equipped to deal with bad weather and could clear the highways in short order. The paralyzing effect of winter in this part of the state did not last for very long. One could be sure, however, that the winter storms were sure to return, and return they did.

Following the storm, I returned to my office the next day filled with excitement about our new ministry. Once back at the church, I found myself busy doing the work of ministry. God was blessing us with wonderful worship services and baptisms, and the budget was increasing. Now it was time to meet with various church committees to plan the work of the church and gear the church for future growth in fulfillment of the vision that I had been given.

It was during one of the first committee meetings that I observed the second storm warning on the horizon. Presented with a sheet of all the church committees by the chairman of the committee that was presently meeting, I noticed that there was not a balanced number of participating church members represented on the church committee listings. This caused me to become a bit suspicious.

By now I was a seasoned pastor and knew that something was wrong with this picture. In a church with more than thirteen hundred members on the church roll, there should have been a broader distribution of leadership and a better cross section of the church's membership representing the church on these committees.

Knowing that it would not be wise to make drastic decisions at the outset of my ministry, I waited until the new church year was to begin before making recommendations that the committees be more balanced by not allowing any church member to serve on more than two committees at a time, thus allowing new persons to be added. I recommended one particular individual, who had financial expertise and who had never been involved on any committee, to be added to the finance committee. This member apparently threatened the status quo of existing leadership and brought to the surface what I surmised to be a controlling spirit.

After that meeting I saw, like the view from our sliding glass doors of a forthcoming storm in the distance, the warning signs of a storm coming in my life and in the church I had been called to pastor. Nevertheless, I had been given a God-size vision for the church and city, and I could not be deterred by threats of a distant storm. A storm on the horizon can be a threat one moment and play itself out shortly thereafter. Therefore, I knew the church must move forward or plateau over a threatening storm that may or may not materialize.

Amazing to me was the fact that not only the church owned the vision I believed God had given me, the pastors across denominational lines owned the vision as well. This was very encouraging to me, a new pastor in the city now serving among long-term, seasoned pastors. Even with all the support, a vision this size was a great undertaking and would require good organization and long-range planning to implement and accomplish.

From the time we arrived on the church field in late October 1991, until well into late October of 1992, things could not have gone better. The church grew numerically and spiritually. Practically every Sunday, new members were added to the fellowship by both baptism and transfer of church letters. But suddenly Carolyn and I were blindsided by a personal storm. I wrote in my prayer diary these words:

> Today was one of the most devastating days of our lives. Carolyn awoke me around 8:00 a.m. to tell me that her doctor had called to share with her the recent results of her biopsy. She said (with trembling voice), "Benny, I have cancer." We embraced and wept together. Most of the morning we cried and talked and sometimes just sat in silence. It took both of us a while to get over the shock.

That afternoon, with fear and trembling, we arrived at the doctor's office to get a more detailed report. In retrospect of that visit, I wrote in my diary . . .

> At 2:45 p.m. we met with Carolyn's doctor in his office. He let us read the diagnosis and then gave us time to respond. His explanation of the test results gave us much hope that the cancer was not widespread, as we had first perceived it to be. We left his office praising God—feeling one-hundred percent better.

Carolyn's doctor was quick to recommended immediate surgery and scheduled the surgery for Wednesday of the next week. What was so frightening for me about this crisis situation was that Carolyn really thought that she would not live through surgery. The word she perceived to hear from the Lord was, "Get your house in order." This caused me to retreat to my prayer closet to pour out my heart to God. I said to Him, "Father, if You need Carolyn, I give her to You, but I think I need her more than You do." I left my prayer room that morning believing that God had heard my prayer and that He would give Carolyn additional days, bringing healing to her body.

The day of surgery came. Carrie, our daughter, had flown from Birmingham, Alabama, to be with me during surgery and to remain through the recovery period. Former staff member and dear friend Pastor Larry Floyd flew out from Indiana to be with us, and many caring, praying, concerned church members filled the waiting room during the surgery. As our friends looked on from outside the waiting room, I gave Carolyn a kiss and watched her go out of my sight, through the automatic doors to the operating room.

Carrie and I made our way to the hospital chapel to pray for our loved one. While I prayed, it was as though I saw a band of angels hovering over the operating table. That was my affirmation that Carolyn was going to be okay. The day after Carolyn's surgery, I wrote in my diary . . .

> "I, the LORD, am your healer" (Exodus 15:26).
> Praise God! Praise God! Praise God! He has
> healed Carolyn. Her surgery was a success, and I
> am praising Him. He has heard my prayer. He has
> seen my tears. He has sent healing (2 Kings 20:5).
> I praise Him!

This storm had passed. That was many years ago, and there has been no trace of cancer in Carolyn's body since her surgery in October of 1992. The year at the time of this writing is 2014. The surgery was among those events that took us into the Christmas season and left us with great expectations and anticipation for the forthcoming year.

Closing out 1992, I wrote . . .

> It is with excitement and enthusiasm that I enter
> the New Year. I am waiting to see what the Lord

is going to do. So, I end this year with a thankful heart, praising God from whom all blessings flow.

I love you, Father
—Benny

CHAPTER FOUR

OUR WORLD IS CHANGING

In the world scene in 1993, Bill Clinton was inaugurated as president of the United States. The Reverend Billy Graham was invited to give the inaugural prayer. "Don't ask, don't tell" would be imposed upon the military during Clinton's administration, along with many other changes that would take place, both for good and for evil.

In the city church scene, city pastors across denominational lines and the churches they led were busy gearing up for a city-wide evangelistic crusade in keeping with the vision to take our city for Christ. Along those same lines, Dr. Charles Stanley, pastor of First Baptist Church Atlanta (Georgia), was invited to the city to do his In Touch Ministry, which would be a prelude to a forthcoming evangelistic crusade.

City pastors were at the forefront, taking on moral and social issues such as abortion, Planned Parenthood, evolution, and other topics that were important in regard to the conservative issues prevailing in our city. Having become well known in the city due to the fact that we were doing commercials on television, I was called upon by the conservative media to address many of the moral issues that emerged during our tenure.

The year 1993 would also be one for doing mission and evangelistic work in the Caribbean, local church revivals, and setting in motion the church's long-range plans. In the midst of all this, I began work on my doctorate of ministry degree. The church, staff, and leadership were so gracious to grant me this privilege. I began this work at their pleasure and with church permission. As a benefit to the church, my doctoral projects would enhance the work of our long-range church plans.

Although things were going well in the church, Carolyn, being the sensitive wife she is to the prompting of the Holy Spirit, helped me to keep things in their proper perspective. On March 23, 1993, Carolyn sent me the following quote from Dr. Charles Stanley's book *How To Handle Adversity,* in which he wrote, "Satan roams around looking for ways to bring adversity into our lives."[3] Thus My question to this was, "Is this merely women's intuition, or is Carolyn so in touch with God's Spirit that she senses a storm of temptation on the horizon?"

Knowing Carolyn as well as I do, the latter is what I focused on. Little did I realize that I was about to face one of the greatest temptations in my life. This temptation, on which I will not elaborate, came on the heels of our highest Sunday school attendance following a revival conducted by a long-time pastor friend from another state.

Our daughter was accepted into the master's program at the University of Alabama, even as a mission trip to Antigua and Nevis, West Indies, was placed on the church's calendar. All this, along with unexpected personal financial blessings, continuous church growth in every area, and a second invitation from International Crusades in Dallas to prepare for a second evangelistic crusade to the former Soviet Union in 1995, was in the making. The church and staff, from my perspective at that time, was fully unified.

I would learn, however, that unity was not the order of the day. Another storm had arisen in our midst. It was the storm of Calvinism. This storm could divide and scatter our fellowship. God, it would seem, was preparing me for the potential threat when I wrote in my journal, God's Word to me today, "Do not be afraid of them, for I am with you, declares the LORD" (Jeremiah 1:8).

In my morning devotional time, I read from Dr. Stanley's book, "The best thing we can do is simply submit to His sovereign decision, knowing that His grace will be sufficient for anything we might face."[4] Taking these encouraging words to heart, I was learning, in the words of Scripture, that "God is our refuge and strength, a very present help in trouble" (Psalm 46:1). Or, in the words of Martin Luther, "A Mighty Fortress Is Our God."[5] Thus I prayed Lord, give me the wisdom to deal with your people who are teaching predestination in one of our adult classes. Help me to speak the truth in love and with gentleness. May the fellowship not be divided." (Prayer Journal, May 10, 1994).

Facing this storm head-on, I met with our minister of education; this was followed by a meeting with the couple who was teaching Calvinism in their Sunday school class. Both he and I confronted the couple and brought this issue to a quick resolve. I wrote in my journal, "Praise God! I believe the Calvinism Controversy at the church has been resolved. My meeting with the couple yesterday brought to an end the conflict."

Although the church conflict was resolved, lines of division had been drawn on both sides of the issue, and the fallout that followed would result in a number of members leaving the church. The saddest part of this controversy was that the couple that had been teaching the doctrine of predestination from a Calvin perspective, and two of our dearest friends, began to separate themselves from us. Ultimately, our once great friendship would end in a broken relationship. It was not long after the confrontation with our friends on this issue had ended that they were reassigned to a new Air Force base, and we have since lost track of them.

CHAPTER FIVE
_____

HOW DOES ONE PREPARE FOR THE UNKNOWN?

Three years and two months were now history in our ministry to the church. The year 1995 was upon us. At this point, it was almost impossible to recount all the great and mighty things God had done in the church and in the city.

In the church, the new church school complex had been completed, the church was debt free, numerical and spiritual growth was continuing, controversies and conflict had been resolved, the church had a regular Sunday morning program on a local radio station, revivals had come and gone, a church anniversary celebration was scheduled, and the list goes on.

God had truly blessed us. In our personal lives, I was well into my doctoral work, and our daughter, Carrie, was having great success in her master's work at the University of Alabama. She had met the young man of her dreams, Aaron Holladay, a student at the University of Alabama. This would turn out to be the young man for whom we had prayed. Wedding plans were being made, and the future looked bright for us all.

In the city, pastors and churches were unified across denominational lines, and great progress was being made in keeping with our vision. Nevertheless, in spite of all the visible signs of a healthy church and a bright future, a major storm was looming on the horizon.

What was happening? The Air Force base, from which about 45 percent of our membership came, was about to be placed on the military base closure list. If and when this happened, it could devastate the church financially. In retrospect, the base did not close but downsized drastically, which affected the church. We lost many military families due to reassignment and relocation, causing the church to make major financial corrections, including a cut in staff salaries. This would happen in 1995. While still a threat on the horizon, that issue would pale in light of the spiritual warfare in which we found ourselves.

It was in light of the uneasy feelings and fears that came from not knowing what the future held for us that I wrote in my journal (using the words of an unknown author), "I know not what the future holds, but I know who holds the future."[6] I did not know what the future had for me, but I knew who was in control of my future. That knowledge belonged only to the One who created me.

Good news came in March about the Air Force base near our city. I wrote in my journal, "Today is a red-letter day. It was announced yesterday that the base is not on the list for closure."

Other good news came from my doctorate of ministry supervisor: my thesis proposal had been approved, and I could begin writing. Although I was really down in January, and on into the first part of the year, things were looking brighter. After having been on a roller-coaster ride for many months emotionally, and having been personally attacked regarding my preaching, I was greatly encouraged when I began getting positive feedback in that area of my ministry.

The research on my dissertation took Carolyn and me to Jacksonville, Florida, to attend a pastors' conference and to do my first interview with senior pastor Dr. Homer Lindsey of First Baptist Church. This was only the beginning of my doctoral research. I would travel many miles across the US to interview well-known pastors of mega-churches before my work was completed.

The conference at First Baptist Church was great, and my first interview went well. We left Jacksonville very encouraged. Now on the heels of a great meeting, it was back to our city of residence to begin serious planning for the Russian Crusade.

Once back in the city, I invited a long-time friend and pastor to be my partner in the Russian Crusade. He accepted my invitation. I did not know of anyone with whom I would rather partner on this mission. This would be one of many missions on which he would accompany me. Also, I began building a strong prayer base among participating church members. By this time, I was feeling good about the way in which things were shaping up in the church. Perhaps this was a bit of magical thinking on my part, but I was very optimistic about the future.

The church moved on to witness the adoption of the 15-year master plan for future growth—a plan that had been in the making by a cross section of the membership, who served on the Long-Range Planning Committee. An outside consultant and close friend did a tremendous job helping the committee finalize the plans. These long-range plans were a major part of the overall vision to reach our city for Christ.

The church seemed to be unified around this decision, but in my spirit I sensed that all was not well. This decision was quite ironic, as the church was now facing serious financial decisions as many of the military families were being transferred.

Be that as it may, the church moved on with scheduled events. The president of Southwestern Baptist Theological Seminary, Fort Worth, Texas, came to lead the church in a revival meeting. The meeting was great, with many decisions being made and a good love offering received for our visiting evangelists.

The revival was followed by my mission to Russia, which was a great success. Serving under the auspices of International Crusades out of the Dallas–Fort Worth area, the mission teams of which my friend and I were a part recorded more than nine thousand decisions for Christ. Not only was God's Spirit blessing locally, He was blessing in some of the remotest parts of the earth.

By mid-September, the numbers were decreasing as more and more families were being transferred, although the baptisms and additions were helping to maintain a balance in gains and losses. Concerning the city churches' evangelistic efforts, many tourists would be in our city for a special event. This gave our city churches opportunity to reach persons from outside our city for Christ. Many of these visitors would be visiting our church on Sunday, at which time they would hear the gospel proclaimed. Our evangelistic outreach was extending well beyond the city proper.

As the gospel was shared during this special event, not only by the church we served but also by pastors and churches across denominational lines, many decisions for Christ were made. Following these special events, I continued my travel, interviewing senior pastors of mega-churches for my doctoral research.

Again on the heels of good news, many of our military families were being transferred and that meant that our financial difficulties would increase. In light of so many families being relocated by the military, I scheduled a retreat with the staff, and we discussed the ramifications of a decrease in the church's budget as a result of so many active giving families being relocated to other bases. The staff was very supportive of me and the decisions we made concerning families leaving the church. I went away from that retreat with a sense that the ministry staff was with me and that the church could survive financially, even if this trend of military downsizing continued among our military members. However, I would learn that this was a mere prelude to the difficult days that were to follow.

The staff retreat gave way to one of the most important events in our lives—our daughter's wedding. Using funds from our inheritance, Carolyn and I put together what we referred to as a

Cinderella wedding for our daughter and the young man she was marrying. Now that we had been in the planning process for over a year, we flew to Birmingham, Alabama, to finalize wedding plans and enjoy decorating the church, scheduling rehearsal dinners, etc., prior to the special event.

The event for which we had waited, prayed, and planned finally became a reality. I shall never forget walking my daughter down the aisle to give her away or having the honor of participating in the wedding ceremony. The wedding was truly a success, and we left Birmingham with a sense of accomplishment at having given our daughter the wedding of her dreams. Prior to our return home, I learned that other church families would be relocating. Following this news, I knew that I faced some serious church financial issues. However, I did not allow this to rob me of enjoying all the events surrounding the wedding of our daughter.

Back on the church front, it was ministry as usual. Returning from the wedding, however, I was confronted with serious budget issues that the ministry staff and I must face. It seemed apparent to us that some drastic measures would have to be made to keep the church afloat financially—even if that meant decreasing the church staff. In light of the present situation, I did something that I do not ordinarily do—I sent out resumes. A number of churches had begun contacting me about the possibility of becoming their pastor, and sending resumes was the way in which I responded.

By this time, the year 1995 was speedily coming to an end, my doctoral work had been approved, and we were getting excited about the newlyweds coming to visit with us at Christmastime.

In retrospect of the Christmas event, our daughter and her husband flew to our home, and we celebrated a wonderful Christmas together. I was privileged to take my new son-in-law on his first pheasant hunt. He was able to bag a couple of nice birds. We enjoyed the day of hunting, but I returned to the church to deal with declining finances. However, even in light of declining church finances, Sunday, December 27, we had one of our highest budget offerings, thanks to our God of surprises.

Another chapter had ended at the church, and we moved forward into the New Year.

CHAPTER SIX

STRUGGLING TO
SURVIVE IN THE STORM

In Mark's gospel, Jesus' disciples are in a storm on the Sea. Jesus, coming to their rescue, finds them "straining at the oars, for the wind was against them" (Mark 6:48).

I don't know of a better way to describe our situation at the beginning of the year 1996, four and one-half years into our ministry, other than "straining at the oars." The winds of change were against us—for the worst, I might add. Things had gotten so bad; survival seemed to be our best course of action against the winds of discord within the body of Christ.

Knowing that a storm was on the horizon, I was reminded of a phrase a former deacon of mine used in closing his prayer. Before the "Amen," he would always say, "And Lord, help us to maintain a good level of survival." That is, basically, where I was in my ministry at that time.

Gleaning a word of encouragement from Dr. Charles Stanley's book, I wrote, "Adversity compels you to grow in Christ if you only will avail yourself of the opportunity to learn and grow."[7] The Lord was, indeed, advancing us, but it was through adversity. The adversity included control and financial difficulties that would eventually escalate into downsizing the ministry and support staff.

This, I believe, was a symptom of a greater root problem: "Who will be in control?" Ultimately, there would be a movement within the church to unseat the senior pastor.

Carolyn and I returned from San Diego, California, in mid-January of 1996; having completed my final doctorate of ministry seminar, I found the church finances spinning out of control. It was at that point that I felt led of God's Spirit to begin a 30-day fast to seek the will of God. I needed spiritual discernment to help me navigate through the storm. I also began a weekly early-morning prayer time with a select group of men in the church. Although I invited the ministry staff to be a part of this prayer time, for some reason they never joined the prayer group. This was very troublesome to me and caused me great concern. Until this time, my relationship with the ministry staff had been very close. We celebrated special events together and shared fellowship in one another's homes on a frequent basis. We played Rook together and shared many wonderful moments on our staff retreats planning for the church's future. It seemed to me that a gap was forming in our relationship and the ministry, which we shared.

In keeping with Scripture, I did not want to make our time of fasting an issue in the church, but I did feel that it was necessary to share with the ministry staff the what, and why, of my time of fasting. However, I did not believe that they supported me in my decision to fast. Nevertheless, on Monday, January 22, 1996, Carolyn and I began our 30-day time of fasting and praying. I wrote of the progression of our fast and what we sensed the Lord was doing in my prayer journal as follows:

> We are fasting and praying, seeking God's will for our lives and for (the church). As of today, we are in the second day of our fast. We are drinking only liquids. Thus far, food has not been an issue since we have been so connected with our present situation. A verse that came to my mind today is as

follows: "And [if] My people who are called by My name humble themselves and pray and seek My face and turn from their wicked ways, then I will hear from heaven, will forgive their sin and will heal their land" (2 Chronicles 7:14).

It is my prayer that God will do a work of humility in my life. I have no agenda for this fast other than seeking the will of God. I am excited about what He is going to do in our lives and ministry. . . . Since I wrote the above words in my journal, Carolyn and I are 17 days into our 30-day fast. I regret that I have not been recording the events as they occur daily.

Some of the inner workings in our lives: Carolyn and I have become and are becoming prayer partners. . . . God has given us strength beyond measure and has sustained us during these days. . . . He has reaffirmed me in my preaching and given me the strength to stand when my flesh would have failed me. . . . The people of (the church) have stood with us in our ministry. . . . The Holy Spirit has given us direction in our finances. . . . Strongholds of pride have been and are being broken down in my life. . . . Material things and the need for them are decreasing while my desire to know God is increasing. . . . My personal prayer life has become more spontaneous, allowing me to be set free of repetitive praying. . . . My (our) love is increasing for the people we are privileged to serve. . . . I am developing a new sensitivity to God's Spirit and to His people. . . . These are among the many things God is doing in our lives during these days.

As I have begun this 17th day of fasting, I am seeking direction for (the church). The one thing that God is leading me to do, at this present time, is to develop a praying church. In the morning, I will be meeting for the first time with a pastors' prayer group made up of select men. I thank God for these men and look forward to developing a wonderful relationship with them.

I am still waiting on the Lord for a breakthrough. Today I am entering my 25th day of fasting and prayer, and my Lord has sustained me. Twenty-one pounds lighter, I have not tasted solid food in 25 days.

Carolyn made this journey with me for 23 days. On Tuesday night, after going to bed, she became extremely ill. I was greatly concerned for her. After a bout of diarrhea and vomiting, she awoke on Wednesday morning very weak. Feeling led of the Lord to break the fast; she began consuming nutritional (non-solid) foods.

Both of us are looking forward to next Tuesday, when once again we can enjoy God's bountiful blessings of food. On this 25th day of fasting, I am still seeking the Lord, and waiting for Him to give me guidance concerning His will for us and for the church.

Last night, February 20, at 9:30 p.m., I ended my 30-day fast. After I came home from visitation, Carolyn served me a delicious bowl of potato soup with three freshly baked rolls straight from the oven. This was a spiritual experience for me. I was moved emotionally even as I awaited the serving of soup and hot rolls. As I ate the food, tears continued to well up in my eyes. I was truly thankful to God for the wonderful bounty of food I was enjoying. After 30 days without any solid food, it was a moment of delight as the food touched my palate.

During the 30-day fast, I continued a full ministry schedule. After three days, the desire for food amazingly decreased. On the 30th day, I climbed a snow-covered mountain, making my way to my favorite praying spot, and spent time with the Father. Coming out of the fast, I suffered no side effects. I was feeling good health-wise, and I was closer to the Master than I had ever been before. I wrote the following words in my prayer journal . . .

Now that I have ended the time of fasting, it is my prayer that I will continue to seek the Lord with all my heart. I do not want Him to stop what He is doing in my life. Thus it is my prayer that the following things will evolve and continue as a result of this time of fasting and prayer:

- Continue to make my prayer life a priority.
- Develop better eating habits—remembering that my body is the temple of the Holy Spirit.
- Maintain the level of weight that I am carrying now—179 lbs.
- Be more disciplined in every area of my life.
- Continue to die to the self-life and take up my cross daily.
- Live in a continuous state of brokenheartedness.
- Be transparent and open before the people I am privileged to serve.
- Exemplify the fruits of the Spirit found in Galatians 5:22–23.
- Continue the growing, close relationship in prayer which Carolyn and I have developed.

As we continued to "strain at the oars," life and ministry continued as additions by church letter and baptisms were being added to the church. Families were leaving the church. Chapters were being written toward my doctrinal dissertation, and the completion was now in sight. Church search committees, along with individuals, had begun contacting me about the possibility of becoming their pastor. The church's financial situation had worsened. The financial committee had met and continued to trim the budget. The attendance had decreased, and the church continued to struggle.

During this time, a lady who was not a member of the church invited Carolyn out to lunch. She chose a place where they were not likely to be seen by any church member. She relayed to Carolyn how she had gone into the sanctuary of our church one time and had felt such an evil presence. She prayed and asked God to reveal to her what was there. The answer came to her, "You don't want to know!" This reminded us of the uneasy feelings both of us experienced when we first came to the church on our initial visit.

It was on an October afternoon during this season of struggling to stay afloat that I met with the ministry staff for a meeting they had requested. It was after this meeting that I wrote these words in my journal: "October 22 was a terrible day emotionally for me. (The ministry staff) met with me in my study during the afternoon, which was a painful confrontation." The painful experience came when the staff with whom I had served for almost five years suggested that I resign. It was due to this painful and hurtful experience that the words of the psalmist came to me . . .

> "For it is not an enemy who reproaches me, then I could bear it; nor is it one who hates me who has exalted himself against me, then I could hide myself from him. But it is you, a man my equal, my companion and my familiar friend; we who had

sweet fellowship together walked in the house of
God in the throng" (Psalm 55:12–14).

Had this been an enemy suggesting that I resign, it would
have been more easily to deal with, but these were my familiar
friends. After this encounter and confrontation, my heart was
deeply wounded after which Carolyn and I talked for hours. Our
conversation gave me a better perspective on what I should do. What
came out of our conversation was that I needed to be more assertive
in my leadership.

That following Wednesday night, God's Spirit gave me the
strength to get through the Bible study. I had been receiving quite
a bit of criticism about my preaching and needed to regain some
composure. The next morning I had a good prayer time with my
prayer partners. Earlier in the week, I had felt a need to fast once
again. On the third day of my five-day fast, I was experiencing more
peace and excitement about being at my present place of ministry,
unaware of the fact that I was merely in the eye of the storm and
that I was feeling a false sense of peace. The real storm remained
on the horizon. As I continued to move forward, four of my prayer
partners were a real encouragement to me. They were used of God,
I believe, to reaffirm me in my preaching ministry. I needed their
confirmation since my preaching had come under attack.

They, along with Carolyn, were my greatest prayer warriors and
encouragers during this time of trial and testing. Carolyn, especially,
encouraged me all along the way. On this particular day, we had
come to terms with "fight or flight!" I had to confess to the Lord
that my fears had made me want to run. I confessed that as sin to
my Father.

On my fourth day of fasting, while at the church, my nostrils
were attuned to the smell of food coming from the gym, where
lunch was being prepared for the students enrolled in our Christian
school. I had a desire for food, but I was not hungry. God's Spirit

was sustaining me during my fourth day of fasting. It was at this time that I wrote in my diary . . .

> God has encouraged me today. He has given me a sermon for Sunday. He spoke to me, affirming me through His Word. My daughter, who had been an avid sermon note-taker prior to leaving for college, also encouraged me. Looking through her sermon notes taken at a previous pastorate from one of my sermons, I was greatly encouraged. Following the reading of her sermon notes, I felt a need to call her and tell her how much I loved her. All of the above is to say, I was looking for encouragement wherever I could find it.

> It is now the fifth day of fasting for me, and I was encouraged by the words I read from Dr. Charles Stanley's book, in which he had written, "...adversity strips away from us everything but Christ."[8]

These words summed up for me where I had been the last year while serving as pastor of my present church. I felt that my work was being attacked, and that there was an attack on me personally, in my innermost nature—my preaching. The thing that had been most difficult for me to deal with was that members of the ministry staff, in my understanding, had misunderstood me. Their words were condescending and cut to my very soul. Nevertheless, I continued to cope as best I could and trusted in the Lord to sustain me.

On this particular day, I woke up early in the morning and spent some time with my heavenly Father, as had become my practice over the years, before going back to sleep for a brief time before beginning my busy day. The sermon outline I had developed for the Sunday message came to my mind, and as I meditated on the text, I began to apply it to my life: "Is this not the fast which I choose, to loosen the bonds of wickedness, to undo the bands of the yoke, and to let the oppressed go free and break every yoke?" (Isaiah 58:6).

My prayer followed . . . "Father, I am asking You to set me free in the areas of my life where I have been shackled. Thank You, Father, for doing so. This is my prayer as I enter my prayer closet on this fifth day of my fast."

On that same morning, I met with my prayer partners who had been a great source of strength and blessing to me. I would learn later, however, that not everyone on my prayer team were as supportive as I thought.

By now the moral of the church had somewhat faltered due to the fact that so many of our church members were leaving. I tried to encourage them through church media, personal letters and through the preaching.

With the help of my heavenly Father, being the sensitive pastor I am, I tried as best I could to release the families that were leaving, emotionally, as well as physically. I thanked God for sustaining me during the difficult days over the past months concerning the issues with which I had had to deal. I thanked God for seeing me through trying days. In every instance and through every circumstance, I have found Him to be faithful.

I prayed to the Father for healing and unity of the body of Christ during the days ahead and to give me wisdom to lead the church body. I thanked God for His continual presence as we advanced through adversity.

CHAPTER SEVEN

A FALSE SENSE OF SECURITY

After "straining at the oars," rowing seemed to be less strenuous now as I found myself in what seemed to be the eye of the storm. It was during the quietness and rest that God's Word spoke into my situation . . .

> Rest in the LORD and wait patiently for Him;
> do not fret because of him who prospers in his way,
> because of the man who carries out wicked schemes.
> Cease from anger and forsake wrath; do not fret; it
> leads only to evildoing. For evildoers will be cut off,
> but those who wait for the LORD, they will inherit
> the land. (Psalm 37:7–9)

In my diary, I wrote, "Resting in the Lord, I now have freedom from this situation. Thank You, Father!"

Resting in the eye of the storm and anticipating more conflict going forward, I became very frightened, like the disciples on the Sea of Galilee. It is my nature to always think in terms of the worst-case scenario. My greatest fear at this point was of losing my pastoral position and having to move from a home we loved without any place to go.

As I fed my fears with negative self-talk, our future looked very bleak. It was now December, the Christmas season was upon us, and I was completing five years at my present pastorate. I said to myself, *I should not be feeling this way*; nevertheless, my feelings were sovereign and I had to deal with them. It was at that point that God's Spirit met me at the point of my need.

I was sitting in my car outside a grocery store, waiting on Carolyn, listening to Christmas music playing from a cassette on my car radio, when I heard these words in the song: "Don't be afraid!" If I live to be one hundred, I will never forget that phrase. God knew what I needed, and He spoke to me through that song. That assurance was followed by words of reassurance from Scripture: "Do not be afraid of sudden fear nor of the onslaught of the wicked when it comes; for the LORD will be your confidence (literally 'on your side') and will keep your foot from being caught" (Proverbs 3:25–26); and "I will not be afraid of ten thousands of people who have set themselves against me round about" (Psalm 3:6). I wrote in my diary, "Thank You, Father, for bringing me through difficult days. Thank You for being with me when I was overcome with fear."

In spite of being in the eye of the storm, the calmness was beginning to be disrupted with more bad news. Decisions that had been made by the financial committee were now being implemented. My salary was cut to the tune of four thousand dollars, my personal secretary was let go, and members of the church came by my study, asking me to resign. What was even more devastating was that my mother, who lived in Tennessee, was critically ill and nearing the final days of her life.

On the wave of the bad news, however, good news was breaking through the clouds. Carolyn, my dear wife, would once again volunteer her services as my secretary. I received word from my doctor of ministry advisor that the rough draft of my doctoral thesis had been approved and I could move forward with the final writing of the dissertation.

The salary that had been taken away was restored to us as a church member counted out $4,100 in hundred-dollar bills and placed it in our hands as a gift. God was blessing us in the storm through extraordinary means.

The good news, however, did not deliver me from the emotional state in which I found myself. December 10–January 4, 1997, would leave a space in my journal without words. It was during this time that I found myself very confused and in a deep state of depression. I found myself making bad decisions at church and sharing things with trusted church members that would come back to haunt me later.

The Christmas season had always been very special and rewarding for my family at previous pastorates. Each December, we would schedule a Christmas party for the deacons and staff. This year was no different. Even though this was not something that we wanted to do, we tried to keep things going on as we normally would. However, the night we were to entertain the staff and deacons, a blizzard blew in and all plans had to be cancelled.

It was during the Christmas season as well that I would do my shopping early for Carolyn, but this year was different. I was so depressed that I called our daughter, Carrie, early in the month of December and asked her to do Mom's shopping for me. A few days before Christmas, the gifts she had purchased for me to give Carolyn arrived. As I was opening the package in which the gifts were neatly wrapped to place them under the tree, I lost it emotionally. The tears began to flow, and I could not stop weeping.

Carolyn, returning from a shopping trip, found me lying near the Christmas tree, weeping, and came by my side to comfort me. We wept together. I continued to be in a state of deep depression for several days, but with the help of Carolyn and a dear pastor friend, along with other local pastors who came alongside me, I was able to win over depression. Nevertheless, by that time I had allowed my depressed state of mind to rob me of a joyous Christmas celebration.

Following Christmas and at the outset of the New Year, 1997, on January 4, I wrote in my diary . . .

> Much has happened since the last writing in my prayer journal on December 10, 1996. Here I sit in my study once again, five days into 1997. I have just finished reading through my prayer journal the words and thoughts recorded in 1996. After this time of reading and reflection, I can say with a grateful heart, "Thank You, Father! Your grace has been sufficient to see us through one of the most difficult years of our lives. I would not take anything for the valuable lessons You have taught me—lessons You are still teaching me."

Getting ready to make a trip to Nashville, Tennessee, to visit with our daughter and son-in-law, I was continuing to thank God for the calmness and peace I was experiencing in the eye of the storm. I wrote in my journal . . .

> Thank You, Father, for the calmness and peace You have given me since my bout of depression last Saturday, one week ago. My circumstances have not changed; in fact, I am (we are) probably facing the most difficult time yet, with my confrontation with the deacons, yet the calmness remains.

Following our trip to Nashville to visit family, and while observing additional blank spaces in my journal, I continued to face the future with faith in my heavenly Father.

Now 23 days into the New Year, our situation was like a roller-coaster ride with its ups and owns. With Carolyn by my side, I was continuing to progress through adversity, knowing that God is faithful and that His grace is sufficient.

Speaking of life as a roller-coaster ride, Sunday, January 23 was an up day. I was experiencing peace in the midst of the battle, i.e., the eye of the storm. We had a wonderful day of worship on Sunday, as I sensed great freedom in delivering the message, and affirmation from church members followed. Earlier that week, I had felt a need to confess to the congregation that I had made some bad decisions, and I asked them to forgive me. After the confession, I sensed great relief.

The next hurdle I would face was a meeting the next Sunday with the staff and deacon body. The essence of the meeting was to discuss calling a Baptist Convention official to do mediation. While that seemed like a good idea at the time, the church was now at loggerheads, and mediation would be too-little-too-late. The meeting went peacefully enough, but there was no resolution, and the mediator would not be called. Basically, we were back to square one in conflict resolution.

We landed back on the upside of the roller-coaster ride when great news came from my doctor of ministry mentor informing me that the rough draft of my thesis project had been approved and was now ready to go to the second reader. So very excited over this good news, I wrote in my diary, "Thank You, Father. I pray that the second reader will approve my thesis, and I pray for Carolyn as she prepares the next set of copies on the computer. God, my Father, You are so good! I love You!"

Time passed as new issues emerged. Friends continued to call in support of us; local pastors and Convention leaders, along with members of the body of Christ, came along our side to encourage us. One of the most meaningful experiences that Carolyn and I experienced during this whole ordeal was when a dear pastor friend, who had become my unofficial counselor, called and insisted that I attend a retreat that was being held in a beautiful setting. He made several calls before I gave in and accepted his invitation. Arriving at the retreat setting, I walked through the doors into the hall where the pastors were meeting, and they were all over me. It was as though they sensed what I was going through. Their agenda that morning focused entirely on Benny Woods, their fellow pastor who was facing difficult days.

During a special prayer time, they had me stand in the middle of the floor as they gathered around me to pray for me. This was an interdenominational gathering of local pastors. The pastor standing at my back with his arms holding me tightly against his chest (while the other pastors were each physically connected around me) prayed, "Now Satan, if you want to get to this man, you will have to go through me!" I shall never forget what I felt emotionally at that particular moment.

That afternoon, Carolyn was invited to join us for prayer, and they continued to pray for us. This meeting got me through the next several days and prepared me for the time when I would come out of the eye of the storm to face the greatest struggle of my life.

It was now February 1997, and although there was still calm in the eye of the storm, things were about to get worse. I got a call from my brother in Tennessee that my ailing mother had died. Carolyn and I called our travel agent, got our tickets, and made our way to Tennessee to be with family.

Many years earlier, my mom had requested that I conduct her funeral. In flight, I reworked an addition to the funeral message that I had prepared three years earlier when the doctor had given her three days to live. She had surprised us all, but this time death in the Woods family had become a reality.

After arriving in Tennessee, while grieving with the family and ministering to them at the same time, God's Spirit enabled me to deliver the funeral message. It was an honor for me to do so.

Even though a number of the deacons had issues with their pastor, they had sent a nice wreath of flowers to the funeral home. The card read, "Deacons and Staff." This was a nice gesture of sympathy that we very much appreciated.

Upon returning from my Mother's funeral, I discovered that other issues had emerged during my absence. Some minor issues had become major issues.

In the midst of the conflict, church ministries continued. The Easter celebration had always been an important event in the church with dramatic presentations. Thus a lot of preparations were being made and many local churches across denominational lines attended our Easter services. By the time the preparation began for the dramatic presentation, the church conflict had spun out of control.

CHAPTER EIGHT

THE "PERFECT STORM"

We were coming out of the eye of the storm. Storm warnings over many previous months had now become full-blown. I was no longer "straining at the oars," I was struggling for survival. I had taken my case to the deacons and had asked the staff to attend the meeting. In retrospect of this meeting, I realize now that this was the biggest mistake I made during the whole ordeal. Having spent many hours in prayer with the Father during these days and months of conflict, I believe that His message to me was, "Do nothing!" Nevertheless, I dared to take matters into my own hands in calling this meeting, and it became a major controversy.

Prior to the meeting, I had prepared as an attorney would prepare for his final argument. I shared with the deacons that the staff had suggested that I resign. As one might expect, the ministry staff presented their side of the argument. In essence, when all was said and done, a clear line of distinction was drawn between the ministry staff and I. The deacons were divided on the issues. Members of the church began to choose sides. Now my greatest fear had come upon me. Would I survive this church storm?

Shortly after this meeting, with the conflict escalating and the shortfall of finances becoming a real issue, another deacon/pastor/staff meeting was called. At this meeting, I made another mistake. The issue at this meeting was *Who will stay and who will go? Will the pastor resign and leave, or will it be one or more of the staff?* I agreed, at the deacons' request, to leave the meeting, along with the staff, and let them make the decision.

I immediately left the meeting and went home. I later learned that the vote was carried out by secret ballot and would not be revealed until the deacons met with the staff and me the next morning, when they would open the envelopes. By the next morning, however, a church member had called to inform me that word was already out. So much for confidentiality!

On a Monday morning I met with the deacons and church staff in my study to open the envelopes. I was not surprised when the contents of the envelopes were revealed. The vote was three to four in favor of my leaving. Of course, this would take a two-thirds majority vote by the church to become a reality.

Since no charges whatsoever had been brought against me the deacons would be hard pressed to convince the church body that I needed to resign.

After the envelopes had been opened, I questioned each deacon, "Do you think I should resign?" Some, with tears in their eyes, answered this question by being non-committal. I must say, this was not a fun experience, but I was able to muster boldness in the face of my opposition. Another meeting was scheduled for the following Saturday night to find out if I was going to resign. During the remaining part of that week, I was consoled and encouraged by some church members and avoided by others.

Saturday came, and I met with the deacons and staff. During the lengthy meeting there was no real resolve in the conflict. I left with the issue of resigning unresolved. I told the deacons that I was leaning in that direction but would meet with them the next morning, which was Sunday, and give them my answer.

After praying that night about resigning, I made up my mind to resign following the Sunday morning message. Early that morning, however, I received a call from a dear pastor friend who had gone through a similar experience, and the advice he gave me was "Don't resign!" I was already in a state of confusion, and now I did not know quite what to do. Again, Carolyn and I talked, and I decided that I would meet with the deacons and staff and tell them that I was not going to resign. That Sunday morning when I arrived at the church, it seemed as though the deacons had deliberately made themselves scarce. There was no meeting. I went into the worship service that morning a bit confused since the meeting I had anticipated with the deacons did not materialize.

That morning, I delivered the message, and all seemed well. After giving the message, I walking down front to receive anyone making a decision, I returned to the podium and asked the congregation to be seated. I then shared with them, without making any accusations toward anyone that I had decided not to resign.

Carolyn was seated in her regular place, and I had prearranged for her to take my arm when I walked down from the platform, and we would quietly walk out together. After exiting the sanctuary, we were waiting at the doors to greet the congregation as I always did after the benediction. It seemed odd to us that no one was coming out. Suddenly, we heard a lot of noise and commotion coming from the sanctuary. Little did I know that this was going to be the worst day of my life.

After a long delay, as the congregation began to leave the sanctuary and make their way towards the various corridors, we learned what had taken place on the inside. I was told that some of the leadership began to explain what had happened when the congregation took issue with them and caused no little disturbance until some degree of order could be restored.

After this, the congregation began to disperse and I greeted people, some crying and others confused. While speaking with one of the deacons, I heard an even greater commotion just down the hallway. The conflict had gotten quite ugly as accuations between church members were being made. Overhearing the accuations between, and among church members, Carolyn, likewise became confused as to what had really happened.

As quickly as she could, she found me and was back by my side. It was out of her fear and confusion she asked me the most piercing question, which escalated the fear and confusion that I was already experiencing. With fear, and perhaps anger, in her voice, she asked, "Benny! What have you done?" I was gripped by fear at her question. The first thought that came to my mind was that even my wife had turned against me. I don't think I have ever been more frightened in my life.

After leaving the building, we went out to lunch with a deacon supporter, and he and his family tried to assure me that I had not done anything wrong. I explained to Carolyn the whole process and line of communication in which I had been involved with the deacons and staff, and she began to understand. That afternoon, after spending some time with Carolyn and the supporative family, I became somewhat settled emotionally, but I would learn after returning to the church that evening for the Sunday evening service that I had experienced only the tip of the iceberg. The worst evening and night of my life was yet to come. I would find myself in the perfect emotional storm.

That evening a Sunday school meeting, which Carolyn and I attended, prior to the evening worship service had been previously scheduled. On our way to the meeting, however, church members who reacted toward us in anger and said hurtful things confronted us in the hallway. In the meeting itself, you could have cut the tension with a knife. I just remained silent and waited for the meeting to be over. Afterward, we made our way to the sanctuary for the evening worship service. The observing of the Lord's Supper had been scheduled for that particular evening. Given the situation, this was not a wise decision. Nevertheless, the deacons and I carried out the service as best we could.

I learned later that one of my supporters had a serious confrontation with another church member while the Lord's Supper was being celebrated on the inside, this supporter and friend of the pastor and the church member who opposed me were close to coming to blows on the outside. I did not learn of this confrontation until some days later. Even apart from that unknown issue, I was glad when the service finally ended and we could go home. I regret to say that our Lord was not honored in that service.

Back in our home and in bed, the darkness of night only escalated my fears—fear of failure, fear of losing my ministry, and fear of not having any place to serve beyond my present ministry should I resign or be forced to resign. The best way for me to describe what I was feeling is that it was a dark night of the soul. I found myself in a maze and saw no way out. Frequent cold sweats, while tossing and turning, caused sleep to escape me. Without a doubt, that was the worst night of my life to this day.

Prior to that dark night of the soul, I was so down that while driving through the hills on my favorite prayer route, I literally screamed out a prayer to the Lord, wanting Him to show me a way out. That was something I had never before done. Now, two weeks later, I got up early in the morning after a sleepless night and went for a drive through the hills. Coming to the curve in the road where I had shouted out my desire for help to the Lord two weeks earlier, I was overcome with a peace, in the words of the Apostle Paul, "which surpasses all comprehension" (Philippians 4:7).

Suddenly, my heavenly Father gave me clear direction, providing a way out of my dilemma, and revealed to me what I must do. My answer from Him was to resign my present pastorate and trust Him for the outcome. The remaining part of my drive through the hills, while returning to our home, was peaceful and quiet.

Upon returning from my prayer drive, I shared with Carolyn my experience with the Father and what I was to do. I had her full support and encouragement in my decision to resign. My next step was to call the chairman of deacons and share with him my intentions. Learning of my decision, he was very cordial and kind, and he explained that he and the deacons would accept my decision to resign and take my request to the church body for a vote. This conversation took place on the Monday morning after the Sunday service in which I told the congregation that I was not going to resign.

I would have to convince my many supporters that this was the decision I believed my Father would have me make and that no one was forcing me to do so. During the remaining part of the week, I made many in-home visits with church members who had been very supportive, explaining to them how I had come to this decision and encouraging them to not leave the church no matter what happened. I followed up by writing a personal letter to every church member, on church letterhead, encouraging him or her not to jump ship.

CHAPTER NINE

PEACE AND SERENITY

Having made the decision to resign as pastor, I spent a relatively quiet week visiting church members and carefully writing my resignation letter to be read on Sunday morning.

It was now Sunday morning, March 30, 1997—Easter Sunday. Between Sunday school and the morning worship service, I made one final attempt to resolve the immediate issues with the staff and spare the church from angry reactions to my resignation. I invited the ministry staff to meet with me in my study, along with one of my trusted deacons. I then proposed to them that I would stay on as pastor, without salary, to help the body heal, and then move on as soon as another church called me. The ministry staff was quick to respond to my proposal, seemingly ready to bear the consequences of my resignation and the immediate and long-term impact it might have on the church.

After that meeting, with the previously prepared letter of resignation in my suit pocket, we took our regular places in the sanctuary. Carolyn was seated on the first pew, where she always sat, in full support of my decision. Following the special music, I stood up to preach with great confidence, poise, and full assurance that God's presence was with me. I then opened my Bible and preached from John 14:1–3.

Following the invitation, I asked the congregation to be seated and read to them my letter of resignation. I kept my remarks on a very positive level and made no accusations against anyone. As mentioned earlier, I had written a letter to all church members encouraging them to stay at the church no matter what happened. The last thing I wanted to see was the church divided.

After reading my letter of resignation, I walked down from the stage and extended my left arm to Carolyn, and together we walked to the foyer to greet the people as they left the sanctuary once the closing prayer had been prayed.

Standing by the main entrance, we waited and waited for what seemed to be ten minutes for the service to be dismissed, until finally the people inside began to make their exit. We discovered later that once I had read my resignation, and before the congregation voted to accept it, a loyal church member and supporter of ours stood to her feet and yelled out, "You cannot let this godly man resign!" That caused quite a commotion, and tempers flared among the folks until the worshippers began to disperse.

To our amazement, as we greeted the members with warm hugs and handshakes, we discovered that 90 percent of the congregation were in full support of our ministry and departed with sad tears of regret over our leaving. The other ten percent, who wanted us to leave, made their exits quickly through the doors opposite the main entrance. After an extended period of time greeting the departing folks, Carolyn and I returned to our home with full assurance that we had made the right decision to resign and fully trusting the Father for our future.

In keeping with the church's policy regarding resignation, I fulfilled my required two weeks. From resignation to actual leaving, the time passed very quickly and was unbelievably peaceful. During that time, the deacon body, made up of both the deacons who were against me and those for me, formed a severance package committee at the request of the body. It was determined that on our last Sunday, there would be a special called business session to hear the deacons' recommendation.

Upon completing my final sermon, as the moderator I stepped into my assumed role and called the church into the business session. The chairman of the deacon committee presented the recommendation. It read something like this: "We, the deacon body, recommend to the church that we accept Pastor Benny's resignation, and that he be given a three-month severance package, with full salary and benefits, and that the church pay a moving company to relocate them to their next pastorate." The motion was quickly seconded, and all was quiet and peaceful until the voice of a newly baptized believer rang out, "I want to make an amendment to the motion!" You could have heard a pin drop.

The amendment went something like this: "I want to amend the previous motion, made to the church, to read, 'This is to be an opened-end motion, giving Pastor Benny a full salary, with benefits, and moving expenses anywhere in the world, until he finds a church.'"

The original motion failed, and then, as the moderator, I called for discussion. Quickly, a voice rang out from the balcony. "I love Pastor Benny," the long-time church member said, "but let me remind you that if this amendment passes, Pastor Benny will never have to work again if he so chooses." Before further discussion could be heard, the question was called for, the amendment was seconded, and the amendment passed without a descending vote. Even the ministry staff cast their votes in favor of the amendment, along with the entire deacon body.

What an ending! What could have been a free-for-all, knock-down-drag-out business meeting ended peacefully. Once the church vote was confirmed, I called for a motion to dismiss; the motion passed, and everyone quietly left the church.

Carolyn and I could hardly contain our emotions as we made our way to the car and drove to our beautiful home that we so dearly enjoyed. Once inside, no longer able to contain our feelings, we made it as far as the living room, where we fell on our faces, laughing and crying and allowing full freedom to our emotions. Finally containing our emotions, we looked at each other and came to the same conclusion: we had been vindicated. We could not believe what the church had just agreed to do.

The days following that eventful, emotion-laden Sunday were relatively peaceful, but very busy. I was putting the final touches on my doctoral dissertation and getting ready for graduation on May 30—and wondering, with much anxiety, where we would go after resigning. During the week following our resignation, a blizzard hit the state, which was a blessing in disguise I might add, because it prevented us from looking for a place to worship on the coming Sunday. During that same week, a denominational leader in our state asked if I would like to meet a counselor and his wife who were visiting and would be in the city that particular week. I quickly agreed for him to set up an appointment for Saturday. The counselor was Dr. Dan McGee, who had co-authored the book *Beyond Termination*.⁹ This book was personalized in our lives when Dr. McGee and his wife came by our home in fulfillment of the appointment.

Both Carolyn and I would agree after our informal meeting with this couple that they were, indeed, a godsend. This couple helped us get in touch with our hurt feelings, gave us coping mechanisms, and helped us overtime to reach our own solutions and forgive those who had hurt us. One thing the counselor said (a statement that had tremendous impact on both of us and one that I have used quite often in my own counseling) was this: "Benny, even though you have cognitively come to a place of forgiveness, it will take your tender, damaged emotions time to catch up." How true that wise counsel was for both of us! My wounded heart would heal faster than Carolyn's, but ultimately she, too, was able to forgive those who had hurt me and come to a full measure of forgiveness. Although both of us remember the pain, the sting has been removed. Our emotions bear the scars, but we have experienced complete healing of the emotions.

Following my resignation, Carolyn and I began to move on with our lives, but the aftermath of our resignation left no little stir back at the church. The church immediately called a special meeting to ask for the deacons' resignation. This meeting took place the day after I resigned. We could only imagine what was going on inside the church building as we drove by to witness an overflowing parking lot. Members who seldom if ever attended the services were called in order to get enough votes to unseat the active deacons.

The end result of that meeting was that not enough votes could be accumulated to fire the deacons. Following the vote, 90 percent of the church membership got up and walked out. That left only 13 families, all of whom had been in opposition to the pastor (see Appendix). About ten percent of the church body is usually the controlling factor. Thus it was a sad day in the life of what had been a great church.

During the aftermath of the mass exit from the church building, many members came to us and wanted us to stay and start a new work in the city, but we were quick to tell them that we could not stay and be a part of starting another church. Eventually, the scattered members would find other places of worship after an attempt at starting a church failed.

As I continued to finalize my doctorate work and get ready for graduation, I found out that a lie had been told that caused some of the issues in the church. The person that told the lie came by and confessed to me what they had done and asked me to forgive them and I did.

After this most revealing day, one of our newest members came by and said, "My husband and I want to give you a gift. We want you to go to a retreat setting and stay in the lodge for a personal retreat." I really needed that encouragement. I readily accepted the gift, packed a few items, and headed for the lodge. This is what I really needed after all the pain and hurt we had experienced at the church. This retreat would be a very meaningful experience for me. While there, I had ample time to take morning walks up the mountain trail to an overlook that afforded me a panoramic view of the beautiful valley and forest lines below. It was there, while seated on a rock and taking in the majestic scenery made possible by the Creator, that healing began to take place in my emotions. Down below, back at the lodge, Carolyn came by for an evening visit, and we sat in the hot tub as the snowflakes fell all around us and disappeared in the steaming water.

One day after I returned from my mountain walk, Carolyn called to inform me that a church in the southern part of the United States had called about a pastor position, and they wanted to have a conference call with me. Excitedly, I left my lodge retreat and returned to our home for the conference call. Ironically, this was a church that had contacted me one year earlier; after I sent all the information they had asked for, the search committee never contacted me again—until now. In retrospect of the meeting with the ministry staff prior to the Easter Sunday morning worship, had they agreed to sanction my request by allowing me to stay on as pastor until a church called, a church disaster would have been avoided.

Little did I know, at that time, that this would be our place of ministry for the following nine years. So much was happening so fast, and it was obvious that our heavenly Father had not forgotten us. After the conference call, I was very encouraged and resumed my retreat at the beautiful lodge the couple had rented for me. I will always be grateful to the family who gave me this retreat. It afforded me quiet, uninterrupted time with the Father and healing for my wounded heart.

All this took place the week after I resigned, and by now we were into the month of April. From April to May, things were relatively quiet on the city front, with little word flowing to us regarding the happenings at the church. The parking lot was relatively empty on any given Sunday, compared to recent days, and we experienced moments of sadness as we drove by. The most difficult part of this sad dilemma was that our vision to take the city for Christ would never be realized, unless God gave this vision to someone else. Nevertheless, our city had been impacted by the gospel. Nothing could undo the fact that lives had been drastically changed for Christ, for time and eternity.

During the ensuing days, as I prepared for graduation, the scattered flock was putting together one final meeting to give us a send-off to our next place of ministry.

In addition to the church from the southeast and other contacts, I had been communicating with a church in our hometown in East Tennessee, who wanted me to be their interim pastor while I was between churches. Not knowing what the future held for us, we put our home up for sale and decided to relocate to our hometown as we waited on the Lord for new direction. The sale of our home is an interesting story in itself. Without going through a realtor, one couple came by and wanted to buy our home, but ran into financial issues. That sale fell through. Almost immediately, however, another couple inquired about our home and made it clear to us that they wanted to move forward with the purchase. The potential buyer asked, "How much earnest money do you need?"

Testing to see if he was serious, I quickly responded by saying, "Five thousand dollars!" He took his checkbook out of his pocket and wrote me a check for the amount requested. Therefore, without our going through a realtor, a cash purchase was finalized. The couple was very happy, and we left the negotiation table with a sizeable profit in our pockets from the sale. This was another indication that the Father was in control of our lives and circumstances. Following the finalization of the sale, we were permitted to remain in our home until after my May 30 graduation, at which time we would call a moving company and return to our hometown in East Tennessee.

While contemplating and mentally gearing up for the move back to Tennessee, graduation day was upon us. Carolyn and I had purchased the tickets for our trip, and on May 29 we packed our bags and drove to the city airport to board the plane that would take us to the seminary where I would receive my degree on May 30, 1997.

During forthcoming days we would reflect on the past four years: the many projects, seminars, and long flights across America; doing research interviews with pastors of mega-churches; and ultimately facing a doctoral committee of three to defend my dissertation. It had been a long, difficult four years, but the reward would be worth it if I could now pass the oral exam.

Arriving at our destination, we were greeted by Carrie and her husband Aaron, along with my older brother, his wife, and two of our best friends in the world, who had flown many miles to be with us on graduation day. It was indeed a joy to be reunited with family and friends for this most important event in our lives. After exchanging hugs and getting caught up on the happenings in each of our lives, everyone checked into their hotels and got ready to spend a wonderful evening on the beautiful campus where I would be receiving my doctor of ministry degree.

The weekend graduation exercises began with the observance of the Lord's Supper in the beautiful seminary chapel; this was followed by a message from God's Word. This was a special pre-graduation celebration for all the students, family members, friends, and honored guests. It was a night to remember, especially for those of us who would be graduating the next day. Since I was still basking in the sunshine of passing my orals the previous day, and having been given the nod by the three examiners to proceed with graduation, it was a special evening indeed. This event gave me hope of a new day dawning after going through a dark night of the soul at my previous pastorate. Borrowing a phrase repeated many times in W. Phillip Keller's book *Thank You, Father,* all I could say was, "Thank You, Father!"[10]

At last, graduation day had arrived. The practice session prior to graduation gave way to the reality of a task completed. Now separated from my family and friends and assembled in a hall across campus, my heart was pumping with excitement in my chest as the invited guests waited anxiously for the procession to enter the chapel. Finally, word was given to take our places as the bagpipes began to play. The processional toward the chapel, where our diplomas were waiting to be received, began. With tassels dangling in the wind and long, black robes flowing with the breeze, a long line of excited graduating students were on their way to a task completed and rewards received. For me, this day was wonderful compensation for what Carolyn and I had just gone through. The possibility of having a ministry in Tennessee, near our hometown made this event even more eventful.

Once inside the chapel, each graduation school was seated according to their assigned places. An atmosphere of excitement prevailed as students waited for their names to be called. Being among the last to receive the special honor bestowed upon the graduates by the president and dean of students, I thought my time to walk across that stage would never come. Finally, it was time for the two doctors of ministry students to receive their degrees. Eighteen doctoral students had started out four years earlier, but only two of us had completed the course and would be receiving a degree.

My colleague and I made our way to the platform and waited for our names to be called. The name of my colleague and dear friend with whom I had studied for four years would be called first, and then Benjamin Franklin Woods. As we stood waiting, the dean of students said, "Today we are bestowing the highest degree this University has to offer on these two students." Then, as quickly as a sword is drawn from its sheath, the name of my colleague was announced and he made his way to the podium to receive his degree. Last but not least, the long-awaited call was made. The dean of admissions announced, "Benjamin Franklin Woods will now come to the podium to receive his degree."

As I made my way up the steps to the bench and knelt to have my colors transformed, the president, diploma in hand, paused, looked at me, and said, "Benjamin! You made it." Knowing that

Carolyn, my family, and my friends were watching and sharing that moment with me, I could hardly contain my emotions.

With diploma in hand and joy of the experience in my heart, I walked off the stage and was later reunited with my family and friends. We spent the remaining part of our time on campus celebrating together.

CHAPTER TEN

TRUSTING OUR FUTURE TO THE FATHER

The day after graduation, we said goodbye to friends and family, left the beautiful seminary campus that I had grown to love, and boarded a plane back to our city of residence to begin packing for our next adventure.

Packing to move out of my church office was very difficult. In fact, it was so emotional for me that I sent Carolyn, with the movers, to pack and on-load my office. After I left the church on Easter Sunday, following my resignation, I never returned.

Our new adventure would take us back to our hometown located in East Tennessee, where I would assume an interim pastorate at a new church start-up My heavenly Father had not left me without a place to serve even after the storm.

I remained there while waiting on our next God-given assignment. It was there, among hometown friends, that I regained acceptance after the rejection both Carolyn and I experienced by members of our church where I had served for five and one-half years. The pace of a smaller church with few demands was just what I needed after a most difficult and hurtful experience. It was here that both of us began to recover from our emotional wounds.

While we were among family, friends, and familiar surroundings, awaiting the church in the Deep South (located "below the bugline," as we were told) to move forward with negotiations concerning my becoming their pastor, our heavenly Father continued to pour out His blessings upon us. The peace that had come following resignation and the vote regarding our severance package was highlighted by, in the words of the Apostle Paul, "the peace . . . that passeth all understanding" (Philippians 4:7). There are no words to adequately describe the peace I was now experiencing.

During a trip to Tennessee to look for a place to live (having left Carolyn to take care of moving preparations at our home), as I was driving through a beautiful mountainous area near the town where I would be assuming the interim pastorate, I saw a sign, which read, "House for Rent." I wrote down the phone number, and when I called later a friendly contractor who had recently completed the building of this mountain house greeted me. I inquired about renting his newly built house and shared with him that we might be there for only a short time, as I might receive a new assignment at any time. He said, "If you want the house, I will ask you to sign a one-year lease—but should a church call you to pastor, I will release you from the lease." We negotiated the payment plan, and I drove away from the beautiful mountain house excited. I could hardly wait to phone Carolyn and let her know what had taken place. This was simply too good to be true; I knew God had once again supplied our need and provided the finances for us to live in such a nice place after leaving the home that we loved and for which we were very thankful.

This was a beautiful home for a couple that was not gainfully employed. After final negotiations were completed between the owner of the house and myself, I quickly purchased a plane ticket and returned to our Northwest home to begin the moving process to East Tennessee.

We endured what seemed like a long wait until moving day finally came on the first of June 1997. Included in the severance package the church provided was the allocation for moving. This gave us the financial freedom to hire the Mayflower moving company.

With the moving truck parked on our property, the movers inside packing, and a home waiting in East Tennessee, we were very excited to say the least. As we sat back and watched the packers moving about and the truck being loaded with our possessions, we reflected on the previous Saturday afternoon, when the scattered church, of which we had been a part for the last five and one-half years, had put together a going-away party for us at a nearby park. The sweet remembrances included the gathering of loving, supportive friends who gave us warm hugs, handshakes, cards, and gifts, along with a delicious carry-on lunch as they sent us off on our new adventure.

The send-off was one that we will not soon forget, but this is not the way we would have chosen to leave. Like previous moves from former churches, this was an emotional one. Prior to the party, one couple gave us a six hundred dollar check, stating that they believe God had great things in store for us. In addition to the four thousand dollars one individual gave us in hundred-dollar bills following the cut in salary, another individual wrote out a check for us in the amount of ten thousand dollars. God provided!

Finally, the moving truck was loaded and on its way to our new, temporary home built on the side of a mountain overlooking a beautiful Tennessee valley below. It was a home we would enjoy for a short time before making our next move to a southeastern state. By the time we arrived there in early June, it was the peak of summer and the green mountain foliage surrounding our new dwelling was absolutely beautiful. We were amazed how our heavenly Father was supplying our need and blessing us in extraordinary ways.

Making sure that everything was in order before handing over the keys to the new owners. The truck was now loaded with our possessions and on the way to Tennessee as Carolyn and I enjoyed some quite time walking through the house, remembering days gone by. When the time came for us to leave, we shut the door, symbolically closing another chapter of our lives and opening a new one. Backing out of the driveway, I said to Carolyn, "Do not look back!" I wanted her to remember the home she loved the way it was before the storm, and to now look to the future, trusting the Father all the way in regard to the new home He had provided.

We drove downtown, spent the night at a hotel, and got up early the next morning to begin our long journey to East Tennessee. We left as we had come, with me in the lead car and Carolyn and Mr. Sam following close behind—only this time, Mr. Sam was wearing a big, white Stetson hat he had bought for himself at a tourist store that specialized in hats. I was wearing a black cowboy hat he had bought for me. We were pretty cool dudes, to say the least, making our way across country on our way to Tennessee.

Although we had left the church physically, we now had one final stop to make on the way out of the city before emotionally closing the door to one chapter and opening the door to this new chapter in our lives. Fifty miles due east of the city is a familiar monument. It was at this monument that Carolyn and I decided to have our photograph made, as we looked back at the city and church from which we had just come, in order to close a symbolic door on a hurtful experience. In anticipation of our move from the church where we had served, we would stop, look back one final time, and make a photograph. We got out of our cars and gave Mr. Sam the camera. He snapped our picture, and we got back into our cars and were on our way to Tennessee. It was here that we laid down the emotional pain and hurt.

Fast forward to our arrival at our destination two days later. We were tired from the trip, but glad to be back in East Tennessee, the origin of our ministry. We caught up with the Mayflower movers in an exclusive housing development, through which we had to travel to our mountain home. Because he did not know how to find our house from this place, the driver had parked his truck and waited for us to catch up. We then led the huge moving van up the winding mountain road, but not without incident. Ultimately, we were able to resolve the difficulties and arrive safely, with our belongings intact, but the off-loading would prove difficult, as the moving van could not negotiate the narrow wooded lane that led to our home. Therefore, all our possessions had to be off-loaded onto a smaller truck for transport to our house. That took some time and energy, but the task was finally completed. Our furniture was now all under one roof.

Waking up the next morning in our new home, both Carolyn and I experienced the peace about which I wrote earlier. Our new dwelling, this beautiful mountain home, was as close to heaven as we will ever get on this earth—at least in our thinking.

For the next few weeks, we woke up to a beautiful forest environment, with the mountain towering high above the city below. Each day we were greeted by a multitude of wildlife: squirrels, deer, an array of birds, and the list continues. We erected bird feeders, bought corn for the squirrels and deer, and welcomed daily all our new creature friends. Arising early in the morning, I would go for a walk through the beautiful housing development below, only to return to our front porch to have a nice cup of coffee with Carolyn and relax and enjoy the great outdoors from our elevated deck perspective.

During the day, and on Sundays, we would leave our retreat and drive down to the nearby town where I was now serving as interim pastor. We enjoyed the slow pace of a small church and ministering to the people that God had given us to serve. Life could not have been better here in our mountain retreat. Peace was replacing the pain, and our wounds would ultimately heal.

Meanwhile, negotiations continued with the search committee from the South, and they invited us to interview. Since the distance was a problem for some of the search committee members, we agreed to meet at a halfway point, at a neutral church where I could preach for the committee and be interviewed at the same time.

Both the trial sermon and the interview went well, and we were invited to take the next step in the process, which meant driving down to the church for the trial sermon. Ultimately, the search process ended, and I received a call from the church to become their pastor. Though we were somewhat reluctant to accept our new assignment, we knew that it was time to leave our mountain retreat and move on to our next place of ministry. Three months to the date (as was originally in the severance package before the amendment passed), I wrote the treasurer of our former church a letter and requested the discontinuation of our salary, as we had been called to pastor a church in the South. This brought closure, and now we were free to move on. One door read "CLOSED, but another, new door read OPEN." Once again, the movers were called, the truck was packed, and we were on our way to our next assignment.

Our new pastorate in the South is a story in itself. Resigning as I did at the previous church, I was fearful that this would damage my reputation as a pastor and that no church would ever consider me to be their pastor. I was hopeful to find a funeral home job at best, or some other secular work, to make it to retirement. That fear did not materialize, and my heavenly Father had a future plan for us. His future plan would be a nine-year ministry at a southern church. During the initial conference call, I had told the search committee my story about the reason for my resignation under difficult circumstances, and they had responded with very few probing questions. Over a period of time, we moved on with the negotiations, and I became their pastor. Carolyn and I will always be indebted to the church for giving us another opportunity to minister. Even though many local churches have gained bad reputations regarding their treatment of pastors who have been fired or forced to resign from their positions, here is one church that took the high road in welcoming this wounded pastor.

Once again on the church field, we were welcomed with open arms by our new church family, and we developed a loving, very special relationship as pastor and people. This southern church would become one of our most successful places of service not as a result of a large membership but as a result of becoming a "sending church" and one that calls out the called. Members who had never gone on mission before joined us on mission to many different parts of the world—Nevis (West Indies), Antigua, Vienna, the former Soviet Union, and southern Siberia, just to name a few. Representing different parts of the world where we went on short-term mission, a section of the church foyer is lined with flags from these countries.

During our nine-year tenure at our new southern pastorate, God raised up numerous young men and women and gave me the privilege to "call out the called," with the church sending them out to be trained and then on to successful ministries. Some were called out as missionaries, others as pastor-teachers or other related ministries.

As the pastor of a sending church, I must share one particular story of how God used this once broken pastor to call out a young man and his wife who would make any pastor proud in the truest spiritual sense. This story is about a young married couple that responded to the call of God to plant a church in the South.

I first met this couple when they learned about a mission trip to Nevis, West Indies being organized by the church under the auspices of the International Mission Board. They were engaged in a profitable produce business. They called and expressed interest in going on mission with us and asked if they could meet with me. At their request, I made an appointment with them, and they came by my church office a short time later. At the outset of our meeting, I was very impressed with this couple and invited them to go on mission with us and serve as our youth leaders. They did a great job on this mission with the youth, so after we returned, I invited the young man to consider becoming our youth pastor and asked him to send me a resume. Surprised by my request, he said, "I do not have a resume, but I will write some things down for you." To make a long story short, over time the couple sold their produce business and became our youth/college ministers. While on staff, the young man asked for permission to complete his undergraduate degree at a nearby university. The church gave him permission to do so, and after graduation he resigned his position and went on to seminary to work on his master of divinity degree. His wife and two daughters accompanied him.

Prior to graduation and just short of earning his degree, he left the seminary at my request and in line with the church's vote to become my associate pastor in charge of youth and college students. My young associate owned the vision that God had given me early on for the church. I can still remember the two of us driving around the city, looking at possible locations where we could start a contemporary church geared toward reaching young people.

While he and other church members owned the vision, the majority of the church did not since it would mean selling the present property and relocating. Nevertheless, the vision did not die; rather, it was redirected. On a Sunday morning, I preached a sermon during which I challenged the congregation with these words: "We can either recoil in fear or respond in faith to God's call to action." When the invitation was given on that Sunday morning, this young associate was on his face in front of the podium. He shared with me later how God had spoken to his heart about planting a church in the South while he was a college student. Having previously ordained this young minister into the gospel ministry during a special called business meeting, the church voted to pay his salary and benefits for three months to help him and his family get started in their new calling.

The rest is history. This young couple, on fire for the Lord, started a prayer group in their home and outgrew the house church in a short time. They then moved their new church plant to a state university campus located in the city in which they lived. They met in the Baptist Student Union (BSU) building. The church grew so rapidly that they soon had to find a new facility to house the many persons who were attending. Now a young pastor and leader in his own right, he and his congregation relocated to a nearby vacant warehouse. It was not long until more space was needed, and the church moved to their present location, a recently closed supermarket, where they continued their contemporary format of worship.

The newly constituted church has since become the fastest-growing church in the city; with multiple staff members and a vision to one day relocate to their recently purchased property in a highly visible location. Meanwhile, the church has opened up another campus in a nearby town.

This young pastor, whom I affectionately refer to as my "son in the ministry," did not "recoil in fear" but "responded in faith." He is being used of God in a mighty way, reaching a multitude of people for the cause of Christ, not only locally but also around the world. In fact, this church, under their pastor's capable leadership, is a partner with a hospital in South Asia (where my wife and I are serving as missionaries as representatives of that partnership). Without this pastor and the church he serves, we would not be here on mission.

I say all this to give God the glory and to thank Him for a search committee and a church that was willing to give a wounded servant, and his wife, a second opportunity. As a result of the church taking a step of faith to call the wounded to pastor, other churches and ministries has become an extension of this southern church.

So, dear wounded servant, take heart. Delay is not denial! God is not through with you. Therefore, no matter what you have gone through, are going through, or perhaps will go through, you are still an instrument in the hands of Almighty God. What He has done for this wounded heart He can do for you.

Our story does not end here, but, having a desire to move on to Section II of this book, I will now cover a lot of territory in a few short paragraphs.

After we had served the southern church for nine years, the members and friends gave us a wonderful going-away celebration. The second part of the celebratory ceremony was our send-off to missionary service. Neither Carolyn nor I hesitate to say that our seasons at all of the churches we have been privileged to serve were positive experiences until our hurtful experience in the northwest church. I will hasten to say, however, we have no sad regrets for having had the privilege and call of God to serve Him in the northwest. Romans 8:28 has been realized in our lives, and we thank God for the experience and for the church that counted me worthy to serve as their pastor for five and one-half years.

When we departed the southern church, once again we were leaving a church family and people we dearly loved and who loved us. Thank You, Father, for the privilege to serve in the South.

Having left our nine-year ministry on the highest note, we were off to Virginia to train and be commissioned as missionaries to South Asia, under the auspices of the International Mission Board of the Southern Baptist Convention. With missions on our minds at what our culture considers retirement age, I took the word *retirement* out of my vocabulary, and we moved on.

We left the church on July 30, 2006 and arrived in India on October 20 of the same year. Our short-term mission trips over the years had taken us to many different countries, with many different teams, and had whetted our appetites and love for missions. From 2006 to 2011, we were on the mission field in South Asia, serving the hospital in the area of pastoral care. This hospital was started by Southern Baptist missionaries in 1973, and has now become a 300-bed hospital with more than a thousand staff members.

Now into its 42nd year as a mission hospital, it continues to grow while doing holistic ministry for the cause of Christ to literally thousands. Carolyn and I are privileged to build on the foundation laid by those who have gone before us.

After three years on the mission field, Carolyn and I came stateside and bought a house in East Tennessee, near where our daughter and her family live. Five months later, we were back on the mission field, fulfilling an additional two-year assignment. After completing our five-year assignment on December 15, 2011, we returned to our home in East Tennessee to do interim pastor work or whatever the Lord had for us at this juncture in our lives. We were ready to settle down and had no more travel on our agenda, but our Father had other plans for us.

For a brief 18 months, we enjoyed life back in America, spending quality time with Carrie, Aaron, and our two wonderful grandchildren, Ben and Audrey. By this time, we had been pastoring for almost forty years; however, it was difficult for us to find a church where we felt at home. After a long search and many visits to various churches, we were led by God's Spirit to a wonderful church in East Tennessee—a sending church. We have known the senior pastor since his early childhood. In fact, I had the privilege to be his parents' interim pastor for a brief time. After several visits to this sending church, we decided that this was the place for us.

Not long after becoming a member of our new church, I became the church's chaplain at the pastor's invitation. I had no idea that becoming involved in my new work there would lead to another assignment on the mission field, with Carolyn and I being sent out under the auspices of our church as missionaries to South Asia.

It is quite interesting how our move back to the mission field came about. It was on an October morning in 2012, while enjoying life back in America, that I received a phone call from the hospital. On the phone was the chief executive officer, who invited me to do an evaluation of the pastoral care department. Responding quickly to his invitation, I said I was more than happy to accept his invitation with the condition that Carolyn could return with me. He readily agreed to that condition, and in January of 2013, we returned to India, thinking that this was a short-term trip. After I completed the evaluation of the pastoral care department and participated in the 40th anniversary celebration of the hospital, and while we were still on campus, negotiations began regarding our return to India to do the same job. Responding positively to his invitation, I suggested that he write my pastor a formal letter inviting us, and converse with him about forming a partnership between the hospital and church.

The CEO did as I suggested, and both my pastor and the church board responded positively. Negotiations began to form a partnership that would end up being a three-way enterprise involving the East Tennessee church, where we are members, the church in the South, and the South Asia hospital, with Carolyn and me representing the partnership under a three-year contract.

After negotiations, and once the Memorandum of Understanding (MOU) had been signed, the three-year contract was put into place. Now under the auspices of the two churches mentioned above, we moved back to the mission field on June 3, 2013 to resume our responsibilities. Now, as I end this final chapter in Section I, we are living a new story.

SECTION II

HEALING OF THE WOUNDED HEART

Having experienced resignation to restoration, I am writing this section of my book as a wounded healer for anyone with a wounded heart, including individuals who are divorced, persons suffering from traumatic experiences or broken relationships, and so on—but especially for pastors, chaplains, staff, and the many others who are in leadership ministry positions. While my wounds have healed, I still bear the emotional scars. And yet, though the emotional scars remain, the sting has been removed. That being the case, I am writing as a wounded healer to offer hope beyond the pain, and to provide practical helps for anyone desiring healing of his or her wounded heart.

In Section I of this book, I tried to show how God's Spirit sustained my wife and me during the trials, and ultimately healed us emotionally. Giving Him the praise, I share with you that there is healing for your wounded heart, and I assure you that you can be rescued and restored, and find complete recovery from the hurts you have experienced. Then, once you have been healed, you can be a blessing to other wounded servants. The biblical principles outlined in this section of the book will help you on the road to full recovery.

It was a well-known American pastor, Dr. Charles Stanley of First Baptist Church Atlanta and founder of In Touch Ministries, who said, "Share in the light that which you have learned in the dark."[1] The Apostle Paul likewise wrote, "Blessed be the God and

Father of our Lord Jesus Christ, the Father of mercies and God of all comfort, who comforts us in all our afflictions with the comfort with which we ourselves are comforted by God. For just as the sufferings of Christ are ours in abundance, so also our comfort is abundant through Christ" (2 Corinthians 1:3–5). Once your wounded heart has healed, you can become a wounded healer to others, as Christ became a wounded Healer to you. In the words of the prophet Isaiah, "By His scourging we are healed" (Isaiah 53:5).

Someone has written, "One of your greatest tests is when you are able to bless someone else when you are going through your own storm."

The basic outline in Section II is used by this author with permission of Basil Frasure, PhD, founder and president of Whole Person Counseling. I have borrowed from his website: www. wholeperson-counseling. The content herein under each section heading is by the author of this book, unless otherwise acknowledged by endnotes. He is a biblical counselor with great discernment and spiritual insight. His website address is wpcounse@wcc.net. A link to his website can also be found on the author's website at www. woundedheart.org.

It was the psalmist who first wrote the foundation verse for The Wounded Heart Ministries: "For I am afflicted and needy, and my heart is wounded within me" (Psalm 109:22). The basic thesis for Section II is, in the words of Dr. Frasure, "A wounded heart occurs when someone or something brings hurt to your emotions."[2] One of the writers of the wisdom literature said, "The words of a whisperer are like dainty morsels, and they go down into the innermost parts of the body" (Proverbs 26:22). As previously noted, I can readily identify with these words, having been personally wounded by a whisperer. Out of that hurtful experience, I came to realize that "hurts never just go away."[3] Therefore, in order to deal with our hurts and the hurts of others, we must first understand a few concepts . . .

THE SOURCES OF HURT

OFFENSES BROUGHT TO US BY OTHERS

Hurt results from offenses brought to us from others (when people say and do things to hurt us).[4]

Since childhood, I have heard the following quote: "Sticks and stones may break my bones, but words will never hurt me." That quote is far from the truth. The late Vance Havner wrote, "Yet words are the vehicle of thought and far from being so plentiful as to be cheap, they are of infinite value. One word can pack more power than a nuclear bomb."[5] Words have power. Words can tear down. Words can damage our emotions as quickly as sticks and stones can bruise and injure our physical bodies. There are three things that can never be reclaimed, as it is rightly said: 1) a lost opportunity, 2) a spent arrow, and 3) a spoken word.

I share with you a personal example. When I was an elementary student in the sixth grade, another student wrote some four-letter words on the blackboard before class. The teacher was very upset when she came in and saw these words written on the board. Quickly erasing the board, she immediately began to inquire who had written these nasty words. She even kept students after class to quiz them. My cousin told the teacher that the guilty party was Benny Woods and that she had seen me writing on the blackboard. The reason this upset me so much was because I prided myself in the fact that I was "the boy who never told a lie," or so the school cook, Margaret Simpson, who gave me that title, must have thought. Whether it was true or not, I liked the reputation that it had brought me among my young peers. Wanting my reputation to remain intact and desiring to clear my good name, I tried to convince the teacher, along with my classmates who were being quizzed, that I did not do what I was being accused of. She did not believe me and said, "Benny, you are not being truthful." I was devastated until the truth finally emerged when a classmate admitted that he had written those four-letter words on the board. Although I was cleared of wrongdoing, the emotional scars from that childhood experience have stayed with me until this present day. I have never been able to delete that painful experience from my memory. The years have passed, but I have never forgotten how that lie hurt me. Not until I forgave the students who caused my emotional pain (as it surfaced from my subconscious mind and I dealt with it on the conscious level) was the sting removed.

While on a business trip many years ago to I met a man who had lost his wife and two sons in a car crash. He shared with me how a drunk driver had lost control of his car, crossed the center lane, and crashed head-on into the car in which the gentleman's family was travelling. With moist eyes, he said, "My wife and two sons were killed instantly, while the drunk driver of the other car was uninjured." He looked at me, and then with clinched fists he looked down and said, "I will never forgive that man!" His hurt had not gone away. Rather than forgive the man who had hurt him, he had buried the hurt deep within and was unwilling to deal with the pain that had enslaved him.

As a pastor and counselor for almost half a century, I have heard this story repeated over and over. The names, dates, experiences, and places are different in each case, but both the pain and the emotional trauma remain for those persons with an unforgiving spirit toward those who have hurt them. Before there can be wholeness and healing over hurts suffered, regardless of the cause or particular situation, the source of the hurt must be identified and dealt with. Therefore, a crucial part of the healing process is dealing with the source of the hurt, i.e., the root problem. That means dealing with the people who say and do things to hurt us.

SINFUL BEHAVIOR

Hurt also results from our own sinful behavior. The following Scripture passages reveal this biblical truth very clearly: "Look upon my affliction and my trouble, and forgive all my sins" (Psalm 25:18); and "He who loves transgression loves strife; He who raises his door seeks destruction" (Proverbs 17:19). In the Old Testament, we read about David's sinful behavior: "Now David's heart troubled him after he had numbered the people. So David said to the LORD, 'I have sinned greatly in what I have done. But now, O LORD, please take away the iniquity of Thy servant, for I have acted very foolishly'" (2 Samuel 24:10).

I have heard it said many times that "every sin we commit has its own built-in death." I have lived long enough to realize this truth in my life regarding sins I have committed. Hurts do result from our own sinful behavior, according to Dr. Frasure, and the consequences can be very painful. As seen in 2 Samuel 24:10, the Lord's judgment was revealed after David's sin. The Bible says, "So the LORD sent a pestilence upon Israel from the morning until the appointed time, and seventy thousand men of the people from Dan to Beersheba died" (2 Samuel 24:15). David's disobedience in numbering the people not only caused him to suffer but also brought the judgment of God upon many others. As Scripture reveals, hurt does result from our own sinful behavior. As so clearly stated in the Evangelism Explosion materials, concerning both God's mercy and His love, "God is a loving God and does not want to punish us, but He is a just God and therefore must punish our sins."[6]

CALAMITY

Another source of hurt comes "from a calamity where one is overcome by the experience."[7] In the midst of his pain and suffering, Job said, "For what I fear comes upon me, and what I dread befalls me. I am not at ease, nor am I quiet, and I am not at rest, but turmoil comes" (Job 3:25–26).

Let us break in on a portion of a conversation that God had with Satan in the opening chapter of the book of Job:

> The LORD said to Satan, From where do you come? Then Satan answered the LORD and said, 'From roaming about on the earth and walking around on it. The LORD said to Satan, Have you considered My servant Job? For there is no one like him on the earth, a blameless and upright man, fearing God and turning away from evil (Job 1:7–8).

The dialogue continues between God and Satan until the Lord says to Satan, "Behold, all that he has is in your power, only do not put forth your hand on him." So Satan departed from the presence of the LORD" (Job 1:12). Now Job would be overcome by the experience over which he had no control. This calamity was imposed upon him.

Job was allowed to suffer at the hand of Satan, under the permission granted by God, as a test of his faith. God was always in control of the torture that was exacted upon Job, and Satan was instructed to stop short of taking Job's life. Beyond that, Satan had free rein over his life.

By way of personal application, there are times in our lives when God, in His sovereignty, allows calamity to come into our lives for the testing of our faith. When that happens, the pain and hurt are no less severe than if we had brought the trouble upon ourselves. However, like Job, the way in which we respond to the testing will determine the outcome of our hurt and pain. Concerning the believer, Paul wrote, "And we know that God causes all things to work together for good to those who love God, to those who are called according to His purpose" (Romans 8:28). We can anticipate good coming out of our calamity. According to this biblical truth, we can know three things in regard to our hurt, pain, and suffering: 1) God is at work, 2) God is at work for good, and 3) God is at work for *our* good. This truth is clearly revealed in the life and experience of Job. When all was said and done, God restored Job's fortunes. The Bible says, "The LORD restored the fortunes of Job when he prayed for his friends, and the LORD increased all that Job had two fold" (Job 42:10). Therefore, be advised by the teaching found in the little epistle of James, who wrote under the inspiration of the Holy Spirit, "Consider it all joy, my brethren, when you encounter various trials, knowing that the testing of your faith produces endurance. And let endurance have its perfect result, so that you may be perfect and complete, lacking in nothing" (James 1:2–4).

Following our difficult days at the Northwest church, God opened many doors of opportunity for my wife and me to serve, both at home in the USA and in some of the uttermost parts of the earth. Again I must say, in the words of author W. Phillip Keller, "Thank You, Father!"[8]

SINS OF THE FOREFATHERS

According to Scripture, "hurt result from the sins of the forefathers as well."[9] Drawing from the Old Testament book of Exodus, we read the following:

> "Then the LORD passed by in front of him and proclaimed, 'The LORD, the LORD God, compassionately and graciously, slow to anger, and abounding in lovingkindness and truth; who keeps lovingkindness for thousands, who forgives iniquity, transgression and sin; yet He will by no means leave *the guilty* unpunished, visiting the iniquity of fathers on the children and on the grandchildren to the third and fourth generation'" (Exodus 34:6–7).

Because God is just, sin and evil that is passed on from the forefathers will not go unpunished. According to Scripture, "He will by no means leave the *guilty* unpunished" (Exodus 34:7).

It seems that the sins of the forefathers are being played out today as we witness the violence that erupts in our American schools, abortion on demand, sexual sins, and all the other evils in our society that will eventually bring God's judgment upon our nation.

DRUGS AND ALCOHOL USE AND ABUSE

In today's society especially, "hurt result from drugs and alcohol use and abuse."[10] The Bible speaks of this very clearly:

> "Who has woe? Who has sorrow? Who has contentions? Who has complaining? Who has wounds without cause? Who has redness of eyes? Those who linger long over wine, Those who go down to taste mixed wine. Do not look on the wine when it is red, When it sparkles in the cup. When it goes down smoothly; At the last it bites like a serpent and stings like a viper. Your eyes will see strange things And your lips will utter perverse things. And you will be like one who lies down in the middle of the sea, Or like one who lies down on the top of a mast. They struck me, *but* I did not become ill; They beat me, but I did not know it. When shall I awake? I will seek another drink" (Proverbs 23:29–35).

Here the Bible gives us a vivid picture of the alcoholic—that is, the one who has become addicted to alcohol. The drug user/ drug abuser not only wounds himself; since the effects of sin are widespread, everyone in his network suffers the pain and abuse as well.

From firsthand experience, I can readily recall the hurt and pain that my family and I suffered when I was a young boy as a result of my father's drinking. My mother, who at that time claimed to be a follower of Jesus but gave no evidence of that fact in her life, hated my father's abuse of alcohol. Although in retrospect I would not consider him to have been an alcoholic, his occasional drinking caused many problems in our family. After going out with his drinking buddies, he would come home with the smell of liquor on his breath; my mom would smell it, and a big fight would ensue. I remember one occasion when the fight got physical. My dad was getting into his pickup truck to go drinking with his friends, and my mother was trying to get the keys from his hand to stop him. In the struggle, he struck her on the face, and blood came from her nose (I am crying as I write); both my older sister and I came to my mother's rescue and separated them. My mom was not badly injured, and this never happened again, but they gave us the scare of our lives. This story of hurt and pain does have a blessed ending, however. Following my conversion experience at the age of 11, and having a tremendous burden for my dad, I began praying earnestly for his salvation. It was some years later, after I had become a teenager, when my dad returned home from a walk along the riverbanks near our home and shared with the family about his conversion experience, which was much like the Apostle Paul's conversion experience on the road to Damascus. My daddy's life drastically changed, and so did my mom's. They began attending church and were baptized. Years later, my dad became a deacon in the church where my wife and I had become members. It was my great honor and privilege to have my deacon dad participate in the laying on of hands at my ordination into the ministry. Again, in the words of W. Phillip Keller, I say, "Thank You, Father!"[11]

As a pastor and counselor for almost four decades, I have seen this drama played out in the lives of many families. According to statistics, more than sixteen thousands lives are snuffed out each year on US highways either directly or indirectly because of drunk drivers. Like the gentlemen recently mentioned, people suffer from wounds for the loved one left behind that go deep within the emotions. If only we could go behind the scenes, many sad stories could be written about the lives that have been virtually torn apart not only by alcohol addiction but also by the use of drugs, both prescription and illegal. Neither time nor space lends itself to further development of many tragic stories the writer has been privy to in the counseling room with families affected by loved ones on drugs.

OCCULT INVOLVEMENT

Hurt results from "occult involvement as well."[12] In the Old Testament book of Leviticus, we read, "As for the person who turns to mediums and spiritists to play the harlot after them, I will also set My face against that person and will cut him off from among his people" (Leviticus 20:6). A classic scriptural example of occult involvement is seen in the section of the Old Testament concerning King Saul and the spirit medium. The story unfolds as follows:

> "When Saul saw the camp of the Philistines, he was afraid and his heart trembled greatly. When Saul inquired of the LORD, the LORD did not answer him, either by dreams or by Urim or by prophets. Then Saul said to his servants, "Seek for me a woman who is a medium, that I may go to her and inquire of her." And his servant said to him, "Behold there is a woman who is a medium in En-dor." Then Saul disguised himself by putting on other clothes, and went, he and two men with him, and they came to the woman by night; and he

said, "Conjure up for me, please, and bring up for
me whom I shall name to you" (I Samuel 28:5-8).

This story continues to unfold in chapter 28 and ends tragically
for Saul in chapter 31, as the sad commentary of his life comes to
an end:

> "Then Saul said to his armor bearer, Draw your
> sword and pierce me through with it, otherwise
> these uncircumcised will come and pierce me
> through and make sport of me. But his armor bearer
> would not, for he was greatly afraid. So Saul took
> his sword and fell on it" (I Samuel 31:4).

By way of personal observation, while serving as pastor in the
Northwest, I read a local newspaper story stating that there were
one hundred practicing witches in the city. That story came out in
the mid-nineties. From my perspective, it would seem that since
that time occult involvement has been on the rise in our nation,
producing hurt in the lives of the multitudes that are involved in it.

The above is a mere thumbnail sketch of the *source of our hurts
brought on by others*. Now we move on to consider...

THE SYMPTOMS OF HURT

Having considered the origin of hurt (with the understanding that
the list above is not all-inclusive and that there are other sources
as well), we must now learn to recognize the symptoms. Often the
symptoms reveal themselves, as the problem while the real problem
lies deep within. For example, the ship's captain sees only the tip

of the iceberg. The body of the iceberg lies deep below the water surface. The Titanic lies motionless in the ocean depths as a result of the unseen portion of an iceberg that was hidden beneath the surface of the ocean. The tip of the iceberg was a warning that a larger body of ice lurked beneath the surface. Like the tip of the iceberg serving as a warning to the ship's captain, so are the symptoms of hurt in a person's life. Therefore, in order to deal with deeply rooted problems, one must learn to recognize symptoms. This is important because, as previously stated, "Hurt never just goes away."[13]

There are three general areas of symptoms: 1) physical, 2) mental, and 3) spiritual. We will consider them in this order. Like peeling an onion layer by layer, the symptoms of hurt must be recognized and peeled away in order to get down to the core (or root) problem; this must happen before the real problem of hurt can be identified and dealt with. This, of course, often calls for a caring friend or a professional counselor or pastor to help one uncover the root problem of his or her hurt.

As a consultant of the Pastoral Care Department at the Bangalore Baptist Hospital in Bangalore, India, I taught Clinical Pastoral Education (CPE—that is, basic counseling skills) to post-graduate students. An important part of that block of teaching is to introduce students to and engage them in the Whole Person Counseling approach, which includes 1) the spirit, 2) the soul, and 3) the body. This whole approach is based on Paul's writing to the Thessalonians. Consider these words in Paul's benediction: "Now may the God of peace Himself sanctify you entirely; and may your spirit and soul and body be preserved completely, without blame at the coming of our Lord Jesus Christ" (I Thessalonians 5:23).

Once I have introduced students to the whole person approach to counseling, I then give them the meaning of Thessalonians 5:23: 1) The spirit pertains to the spiritual part of man and involves a relationship with God and other spiritual beings, 2) the soul pertains to the psychological and social aspects and involves the mind, will, and emotions, and 3) the body pertains to the physical part of man and involves the senses of hearing, seeing, smelling, tasting, and feeling (Frasure). Without understanding the whole-person, biblical approach to counseling, the counselor can only provide, at best, a "Band-Aid" service to the client. Without the counselor understanding this biblical approach and properly applying it, physical symptoms, mental symptoms, and spiritual symptoms can never adequately surface in the client and be adequately dealt with.

Having laid this groundwork, we will now take a look at the three areas of symptoms:

PHYSICAL SYMPTOMS

The writer of Proverbs wrote, "A joyful heart is good medicine, But a broken spirit dries up the bones" (Proverbs 17:22). Writing of hurt produced by sin, David wrote in the Old Testament, "When I kept silent *about my sin* my body wasted away through my groaning all day long. For day and night Your hand was heavy upon me; My vitality was drained away *as* with the fever heat of summer" (Psalm 32:3-4). The sin about which David "kept silent" was the one he committed with Bathsheba, written about in 2 Samuel, beginning in chapter 11. It was about David's repentance, which we read about in Psalm 51, that he was forgiven and rediscovered the joy of the Lord. He started on the road to recovery from his hurt, which was self-inflicted, only after Nathan's rebuke.

Having heard Nathan's story of the ewe lamb, David responded out of anger:

> "Then David's anger burned greatly against the man, and he said to Nathan, As the LORD lives, surely the man who has done this deserves to die. He must make restitution for the lamb fourfold, because he did this thing and had no compassion. Nathan then said to David, You are the man! Thus

says the LORD God of Israel, It is I who anointed
you king over Israel and it is I who delivered you
from the hand of Saul" (2 Samuel 12:5-7).

This story of David picks up in Psalm 51. After taking
responsibility for his sin, David prays, "Against You, You only, I have
sinned and done what is evil in your sight, So that You are justified
when You speak and blameless when You judge" (Psalm 51:4). We
know the rest of the story. God forgave David, but he had to suffer
the consequences of his sin.

David's problem began with the physical, but could not be dealt
with at that level alone. His problem lay deeper. It was spiritual.
He had broken relationships with both God and significant others.
He was brought to his senses in the soul area of his being (which
pertained to the psychological and social aspects of his being) by
Nathan. Therefore, in a counseling situation, the counselor must
probe, under the power of the Holy Spirit, until he reaches deep
within the client to the level at which the root problem is revealed.

Many hospital beds are occupied by patients suffering from the
physical symptoms listed below. According to the medical profession,
though symptoms reveal themselves in these various forms, the root
problem may very well be psychological (Frasure).

- Nerve Disorders
- Allergies
- Stomach Problems
- Heart Aches
- Insomnia

That is why, at the Bangalore Baptist Hospital, holistic healing
is provided through the medical staff and chaplains, as stated in our
mission statement, which promises "Healing and Wholeness in the
Spirit of Jesus Christ." While many symptoms of our patients are
physical and are treated by our medical doctors, our chaplains look

beyond the physical to the spiritual and psychological needs that lie deep within and that are a result of deep hurts and wounds in the patients' lives, which have occurred in the past. These physical symptoms may, in fact, reveal themselves as nerve disorders, allergies, stomach problems, heartaches, and insomnia. Our job as chaplains is to provide assistance in keeping with the five traditions of pastoral care as exemplified in the life and ministry of Jesus: reconciling, nurturing, guiding, sustaining, and healing. The aim of the pastoral caregivers is to go beyond the physical symptoms (leaving that to the medical profession) and search for deeply rooted psychological, emotional, and spiritual problems through the use of probing and other counseling methods.

MENTAL SYMPTOMS

In the wisdom literature we find these words: "The spirit of a man can endure his sickness, But as far a broken spirit who can bear it" (Proverbs 18:14).

It was due to my personal encounter with rejection and broken relationships at the previously mentioned church that I experienced some of the symptoms listed below, including depression and confusion.

Depression

Carolyn saw the symptoms of depression long before I became aware that I was depressed. This was in 1996, just before Christmas and prior to my resignation on Easter Sunday in 1997. As explained in a previous chapter, one Saturday afternoon, after receiving gifts in the mail that our daughter Carrie had purchased for me to give Carolyn, I lost it emotionally. As I opened the package and started to put the gifts under the Christmas tree, a flood of tears began to stream down my face. I wept uncontrollably for at least two hours. Carolyn tried to console me as best she could until that bout of depression ran its course. In the words of the writer of Proverbs, I was mentally and emotionally suffering from a "broken spirit." Two dear pastor friends came alongside me over the next few weeks to help me through my depressed state of mind.

Fits of anger and rage

I did experience some degree of anger toward the church members and staff who called upon me to resign as pastor, but was able to deal with it on a conscious level and resolve the issue quickly. With the help of God's Spirit and concerned counselors, I did not allow my anger to turn into rage.

Confusion

Confusion, however, was another issue. On several occasions during the heat of battle, I became very confused. The most noticeable symptom was that I had difficultly making decisions. When I did make a decision, I would immediately begin to question myself about the validity of my decision. I would tell one church member one thing and another member something else, forgetting what I had told the first person. Being in a state of confusion at times got me into a lot of trouble.

Various Fears

I certainly had fears of the future. I was afraid that if I were forced to resign as pastor, no other church would consider me. Fear of an uncertain future gripped me in a powerful way. The fears I experienced would assail me in various ways. To this day I still have fear of losing something or someone that I hold dearly.

Shyness

Although I did not experience shyness, my introverted personality escalated to new heights. Frequently, and at various times, I just wanted to withdraw and be left alone.

Dominance

There were times when I tried to dominate by taking matters into my own hands. This was a method I used to protect myself from further hurt.

SPIRITUAL SYMPTOMS

The evangelist Matthew had this to say: "And his lord, moved with anger, handed him over to the torturers until he should pay all that was owed him" (Matthew 18:34).

Nightmares

It has been said about dreams by an unknown author, "Dreams are the symptoms of a deeper problem, and a product of guilt." Though I know very little about dreams and the interpretation thereof, I would venture to say that this quote is fairly accurate. People suffer from many spiritual symptoms of deeper problems that are buried deep within the subconscious mind and that stem from guilt, often revealing themselves as nightmares.

Hearing voices

Other spiritual problems will manifest themselves in the hearing of voices. This is especially true of persons who are contemplating taking their own lives. When a person reaches this stage of clinical depression (brought on by hurt, rejection, failure, a crisis situation, etc.), drastic steps must be taken to help, especially when the person has reached the stage of hearing voices.

Seeing unusual things

Spiritual issues also reveal themselves in the lives of persons who are in a crisis situation or suffering from some deep emotional wound. Seeing unusual things, for a person in an emotional crisis, may appear as a moving object in the darkness, and suddenly disappear. In reality the moving object, or shadow, may only have appeared in their imagination, but was very real to them.

Lack of control of self

This is also a symptom of a spiritual problem. The person who is suffering from deep, emotional wounds and hurt quite often experiences this symptom. The symptom of lack of self-control may often come in the form of a temptation. For example, a woman who is deeply hurt by a husband who has rejected her may be tempted to find acceptance in the arms of another man. A pastor who has been hurt by his church family may be tempted to leave the ministry, even though the call of God is very real in his life, because he feels that he has failed. In both cases, there is a lack of self-control due to the trauma they are experiencing.

While symptoms of hurts, brought on by others, reveal themselves as above, persons who have been hurt deal with their hurts in various ways. Thus we will consider...

WAYS IN WHICH PEOPLE RESPOND TO THEIR HURTS

Now that we have considered the symptoms of hurt, let's consider the ways in which people respond to hurts.

ANGER

Anger is one way in which a person responds to hurt. It was during a counseling session that I witnessed an outburst of anger from a client who had undergone a painful experience many years ago. They had not learned to cope with their anger effectively. It became apparent to me that I was dealing with an angry person early on in the counseling session. As I began probing in search of the deeper-rooted problem the client went into a fit of anger, turning their anger outward. All the symptoms of anger began to emerge, being manifested in the tightening of the face muscles, snarling and gritting of their teeth like a mad dog, clenching of their fists, and raising of their voice. The session ended on a bad note, with the root problem still submerged. Tragically, this client is still responding to their hurt in the best way they knows how, out of the anger that is buried deep within.

Hurt that is not dealt with will eventually lead to anger. It was uncontrolled anger that led to the first murder in the Bible. Cain, the eldest son of Adam and Eve (the first man and woman created), killed his brother Abel. The Biblical account reads as follows:

> "So it came about during the course of time that Cain brought and offering to the LORD of the fruit of the ground. Able, on his part also brought of the firstlings of his flock and of their fat portions. And the LORD had regard for Abel and for his offering;

but for Cain and for his offering He had no regard. So Cain became very angry and his countenance fell. Then the LORD said to Cain, Why are you angry? And why has your countenance fallen? If you do well, will not your *countenance* be lifted up? And if you do not do well, sin is crouching at the door; and its desire is for you, but you must master it. Cain told Able his brother. And it came about when they were in the field, that Cain rose up against Abel his brother and killed him" (Genesis 4:3-8).

The anger of Cain against his brother Abel led to the first murder in the Bible.

BITTERNESS

Bitterness, accompanied by anger, is another way a person can respond to their hurt. As seen above, when hurt is not dealt with effectively and appropriately, the anger will move to the next level—bitterness. Life hurts will make a person better or bitter. It depends on how a person responds to their hurt. I counseled a person who is retired and seemingly not at peace. This person is suffering from previous hurt—hurt that has turned into bitterness over the years. Because they buried their hurt and pain deep within, they have developed an unhealthy coping mechanism that isolates themself from significant others. During the counseling session, the counselee shared with me the details of their hurt and pain. As they did so, I detected an unforgiving spirit. Though I offered the counsel that would set them free from their unforgiveness toward the person who had hurt them they chose rather to hold on to the bitterness and what I surmised to be deeply rooted. A symptom of the bitterness is now being displayed toward significant other persons. They shield themselve from further hurt by trying to control the persons around them.

HATRED

The anger of Cain against his brother Abel led to hate, and he killed him.

Similar tragic stories are repeated daily in various cultures around the world. Unresolved anger is like a powder keg waiting for the spark that will ignite it. Unresolved anger does not lie dormant. It feeds on bitterness, blaming others, and ultimately leads to hatred. Hatred then goes beyond simply blaming others to the desire for "a pound of flesh," often unleashing itself as revenge.

REVENGE

Revenge is always destructive at best. Our American society has become too familiar with road rage. It is not unusual to pick up the morning newspaper, or turn on the television, and read or hear about a murder on the highway as a result of road rage. One driver unintentionally cuts off another driver, eye contact is made, words of profanity are shouted at the innocent driver—who is then forced off the road, the innocent driver reacts in kind to the angry driver, shots are fired, and a man lies dead beside the highway.

FEAR

Fear is a normal human emotion, but fear driven by anger can become deadly. For example, fear of being hurt again can lead a desperate man who has gone through a bad divorce to kill the wife he once loved to keep her from hurting him again. This, of course, is a hypothetical example, but has been played out in the real world. Again, "hurt never just goes away."[14] It must be dealt with, and if it is not, it will be revealed through one's personality and behavior as anger, bitterness, hate, revenge, and fear.

Suffice it to say, in light of the above list, (ways in which people respond to their hurts), that not all people respond to their hurt in the same way. I now share with you a beautiful letter written by a wounded pastor's wife (and used by permission) that reveals so candidly how she responded to her hurt. In this letter, she opens up her heart in a testimony depicting how she dealt with pain and suffering at the hands of others. She further reveals how God used these undesirable circumstances in her life to mold her into the person she is becoming.

The Wounded Pastor's Wife

If you are reading this, I imagine two things about you: 1) you are a pastor's wife, and 2) you are a wounded pastor's wife. So am I.

When Benny asked me to write this article, I did not want to at first. Oh, I have written volumes in the past year in my journals and in communication with a few trusted family and ministry friends since God finally released my husband and me from the most painful situation in all his 28 years of ministry. But as we neared the first anniversary of his resignation and departure from the church, I just did not want to rehash, one more time, all the tricks, lies, hostility, and hatred that developed over a four year period, and escalated into a three-year battle. This battle almost destroyed us during our final five-month onslaught of hell. Nevertheless, for the past couple of weeks, I have felt nudged by the Holy Spirit to write something. Three very lengthy attempts later, I finally realized that I was writing about the wrong thing. It became clear to me that you, the reader, have neither the interest nor the emotional resources to read all about anyone else's sufferings at this point in your life.

What you *do* need to read is this: (1) It is okay for you to hurt, to be angry, to feel all the emotions which you may have previously thought only unsaved people, certainly not Christians, would go through in a time of crisis. (2) I encourage you to accept the provision from the Lord of two or three trustworthy and "safe" people with whom you can vent and empty out your heaped-up emotional pile. You need Spirit-filled listeners to help dissipate some of your pain. (3) It is not surprising if some of your anger is aimed at God Himself. He can take it, and hopefully your "listeners" will understand and be patient with it, too. (4) Realize that you may sink even lower than you are right now in body, mind, emotions, and spirit before you begin to heal. (5) Take the time you need *now* to process through all you have experienced and have been so deeply wounded by. (6) In spite of everything in your heart and mind telling you otherwise, you will recover. Your life circumstances may be different in the future than they have been in the past, but that which is truly "you" will recover and remain. (7) It is possible that your greatest days of joy and usefulness to God's kingdom are still ahead of you—maybe in the pastorate, maybe not—and they will perhaps be *the best* days of your life and the most fruitful for God's kingdom.

I know all about the grief cycle—I had taken a seminary course in it and had lived through grief resulting from the deaths of loved ones and from various other painful situations, which had happened, to my husband or to me in our 36 years of marriage. But I didn't recognize until very recently that the overwhelming process I was going through as a consequence of years in a dysfunctional ministry environment and our subsequent departure from it was profound grief . . . absolute, all-encompassing, disabling grief. There were days when I thought the world had moved on and left me far behind. I didn't think I would ever be able to catch up with loved ones' lives or that it would be possible for us to have a real life of our own again. Nothing was beautiful, lovely, sweet, joyous, or warm to me. I was living in a cold, harsh, gray world. It was like no one's love or care could touch my heart. I began to wonder if I was having an emotional breakdown.

I know that I did *not* have a spiritual breakdown! It finally dawned on me that the reason I was consumed with replaying and rehashing and rethinking incident after incident of our years of struggle was that I was desperately searching for evidence that God truly had been accomplishing something positive for someone as a result of our misery—but I couldn't see it. Perhaps, God was defending us, protecting us—at least rescuing us. I had assumed that we must deserve the sick, passive-aggressive hatred heaped upon us for some reason we could not comprehend. That's when I finally began to seriously question if I wanted to stay in communication any more with God if He was like that. I was *really* hurt by what He allowed to happen to us without giving us a clue as to *why* He was doing it. *When* and *what* did we do to so fail God and others that we should have become the brunt of this venomous pursuit, this cleverly woven web of accusation and suspicion? As you can see, I was severely negatively impacted.

Of course, this is what Henry Blackaby calls "a crisis in belief."[15] I knew all that—I had *taught* it for many years in Sunday school classes and Bible study groups. I knew I had experienced several tests and trials in many decades of life, and I appeared to have survived intact. I presumed I always would. After all, I was from hardy stock regarding my family, and in my faith I was a veteran overcomer in many circumstances: resilient, experienced, strong. Everyone else expected me to keep getting up, dusting myself off, and jumping back into that ring—and no one expected it more than I did. But *nothing* like what we were experiencing at this church had ever come our way before. And I began to doubt if I would survive this "crisis of belief," or possibly even life itself.

As I look back now, I can clearly see that our journey was the one you read about in the Footsteps poem. The Lord was clearly carrying us through those years of relentless attack, which escalated from just wanting us gone from that church to obviously wanting us to be destroyed. But at that time, as we lived in the tumult day after day and as I was trying to recover from the resultant wounds, I just could not sense that the Lord's presence or love or care had been there with us. My hurt and insecurity and sense of abandonment were too deep.

I tried to read my Bible and devotions (I couldn't concentrate long enough to read chapters in books). Bit by bit, piece by piece, months later in the warm, loving, safe environment of our parents' home (and later, our children's home), the Still Small Voice began to reach me. I responded with much anger and bitterness for quite a while, but He kept sending His love message to me in a variety of ways and through various people.

Slowly, the verse I had staked my life on, which says, "I will be with you; I will not fail you or forsake you" (Joshua 1:5), for so many years and even used to lift others up began, once again, to be meaningful to me. It took months, don't get me wrong, but I began to trust the promises in old familiar verses, and new ones became crystal clear and momentous. I still occasionally tried to demand answers to questions like *Why, God?* Why did You let those *so-called Christians* do this to us-and to several of the precious pastors as well-and what about those *yet* to come?" How could all this bring glory to You and advancement to your Kingdom? Who, Who is better because of this?" Gradually those questions became statements such as *I have* hated what we have been through, Lord, I don't think I will ever be fully recovered or that I will be "myself" again, but I do know that somehow someday, something worthwhile will come out of this."

Of course, I had long known about "the fellowship of the suffering saints," but that concept in the midst of the battle did nothing but heap fuel on my fires of indignation. I was ready for "those people" to experience some of "the fellowship of suffering" for a while instead of the victory dance they were enjoying! Where was God when one of the most courageous and faithful servants, my husband and my pastor, was being treated like (and being thought of as) the scum of the earth? *What was going on?*

Here's the part I don't really want to tell you: to this day, to my knowledge, the Lord has *not* answered any of my questions I demanded of Him, nor has He acted on any of my desires for His swift and sure judgment and punishment of the offenders. But please keep reading. What *has* happened is that very slowly—amidst huge doses of love and support from our families; through calls, visits, and hugs from ministry friends sprinkled all throughout the past year; from reading countless love notes from the Lord in Scriptures or articles we "happened" to find here and there; from the lyrics of songs we heard on the radio or CDs; from personal messages in sermons we were in the right place at the right time to catch; from testimonies amazingly aired on secular channels as well as Christian stations; and through many more avenues, the sometimes still painful healing process began.

I cannot recall exactly when or how I started to believe that we could "live again,"[16] as Catherine Marshall wrote so many years ago. It must have occurred sometime during the appearance of two new ministry opportunities for my husband; the miraculous purchase of our house and relocation to the same city where our children were; the discovery of an incredibly loving, prayerful, wise "pastor of the wounded heart" in a small church with a big heart in the neighborhood; and many more pieces of the puzzle which gradually put our lives back together.

Healing was also the result of the conscious, willful decision many times over by my husband and by me to declare that we forgave these individuals . . . name by name. Every time my husband or I perceived lingering desires for them to hurt like we had been hurt by them, we would verbally express our release of that desire for revenge and give their lives, their futures, and their offenses against us over to God for *His* just and righteous dealings. (And we resisted the temptation to give Him our suggestions on that subject!)

Quite surprisingly to me one day, I realized that these people, who during three years had grown to loom so huge in my mind and emotions that they obliterated almost everything and everyone else, had now begun to shrink in my mind's eye. Once I realized that fact, I made a conscious effort to *use* that concept to help my sanity return. I drew pictures of how big those people used to be in my mind and life in relation to God, my husband, our family, our friends, and our life otherwise. Slowly, as the days passed and I drew again and again, those people grew smaller and smaller as God once again resumed His place in my heart and mind. My loved ones again occupied their rightful places of priority in my thinking and doing. Instead of a melted puddle, I was standing tall again and smiling. And now, I have recovered enough to begin opening up my circle to let new people in, even some with their own ongoing hurts and suffering.

I don't have a deep wellspring to minister to them like I used to. I am still vulnerable and have to pull back quickly when I realize I am on shaky ground. But I have gained enough strength to feel confident that I will be "thoroughly furnished for every good work" again one of these days.

Have I been able to pray good things for our attackers' lives? Have I been able to pray that God will lavish blessing upon those who abused us? No. Have I been able to think of them with fondness and look back to the good times before they turned on us, to the shared ministry with them, to the crises in their lives that my husband and I ministered to them through—instead of recalling what they did to him? Only rarely, and then with great sorrow. I have recognized that it takes God Himself to be able to change the bitter to sweet. It takes someone with a heart as big as Jesus' heart to be able to completely erase all record of wrongs. I can only hope and pray those realities will be achieved some day in my heart and mind.

After much prayer, however, I sense that it is okay that I don't have gushy, mushy loving feelings for those folks or that I don't desire to fellowship with them again. It is sufficient that they no longer occupy my every waking thought—that I have, as an act of my will, given up the right to get even with them and have placed them in God's hands. It is enough that I no longer remind God of their list of offenses against us so He will make judgments about them that would appease my scarred flesh. It is enough that I am now able to look around and see the Lord's loving hand in my life again. It is enough that I am, though still weakened, gaining strength daily. It is marvelous indeed that my husband and I are enjoying more free time together than busy schedules previously allowed, and that we are having more opportunities to be with our family than we ever dreamed we'd have—what a blessing! My husband is relishing fresh and varied ministry opportunities. And most doors are opening to him. Life has again become an adventure in the Lord.

So, Dear Sister, without you knowing the details of our journey and without me knowing the details of yours, I still can confidently declare to you—you will survive! The Lord *is* on your side! He has *never* left you nor forsaken you, and if you can't feel Him right now, don't give up! He *is* there— constantly interceding and providing for you. One day soon those walls of defense you built up to keep out the bandits and the pain they inflicted upon your husband and you and your children—those walls will be able to come down, and you will again see the faces of all who love you and are there for you, and you will know that the Lord truly was with you through your valley and shadow of death.

You have just read the testimony of a wounded pastor's wife regarding her hurt and pain and subsequent recovery. The candid unveiling of her journey through the valley of emotional suffering and the way in which she dealt with her hurt gives us all hope that there is peace beyond the pain. Our recovery from hurt (as "hurts never just goes away"[17]) and the manner in which we deal with the hurt makes all the difference. When people say and do things that hurt us, we must find the right coping mechanism to get us through the moment and to sustain us during the journey to full recovery, as the pastor's wife did. Often times, in defense of the loved one that was hurt, the significant other receives the brunt of the pain and finds it even more difficult to forgive the person, or persons, who delivers the pain. This was true in my wife's case as she came to my defense when I was under attack. Long after I had forgiven those who hurt us and moved on emotionally, her emotions had still not caught up with her choice to forgive. Yes, the scars remained for me, but my emotions had healed and were no longer tender from the pain. Did I forget what both of us had gone thorough? Definitely not, but the sting had been removed and I could move on with my life.

Having considered how people respond to their hurts, let us recognize that responses fall into one of two categories. According to author Scott Floyd, PhD, associate professor of psychology and counseling at Southwestern Baptist Theological Seminary, Fort Worth, Texas, we can respond with Effective Coping or Ineffective Coping. In his book *Crisis Counseling*, he writes the following:

> Individuals who do well in the aftermath of crisis, trauma, or loss seem to find ways to cope effectively. Whether they do intuitively, through reading and learning about coping, or through the use of available support, they seem to adjust. If they've faced a significant trauma or loss, effective coping generally involves going through the grieving process. These individuals are able to successfully separate from the losses they've experienced and are prepared to function productively in both the present and the future.[18]

Borrowing from Dr. Scott's book, I have charted his model of both Effective Coping and Ineffective Coping and the various stages the hurting person may go through:

Effective Coping:

- Adjustment to losses
- Utilization of support
- Appropriate grief
- Appropriate depression
- Accurate view of God

Ineffective Coping:

- Regret
- Blame
- Bitterness
- Depression
- Magical thinking
- Incomplete grieving

According to Dr. Scott's model, as this author sees it, the way in which a hurting person responds to their circumstances will make all the difference in their journey through the emotional pain, and eventually to full recovery.

Not only can we use effective coping in response to our hurts, we can eventually find healing and wholeness for our damaged and wounded emotions. This is made possible through God's provisions. I like the way Paul said it in his letter to the Philippians: "And my God will supply all your needs according to His riches in glory in Christ Jesus" (Philippians 4:19).

Using Dr. Scott's model, I will attempt to show how a terminally ill cancer patient responded to his physical pain and suffering as well as his emotional pain due to the loss of his career and his inability to travel and do the things he once enjoyed. As you will see from his story, he adjusted to his losses, utilized support, experienced appropriate grief and depression, and—although suffering continuous pain— maintained an accurate view of God.

I met Wilfred Lloyd Laffernis in 2007, while he was a patient in the Intensive Care Unit at the Bangalore Baptist Hospital, Bangalore, India. My wife and I had just arrived on the mission field in late October of 2006, and were assigned to the hospital. One afternoon as I made my hospital rounds (being new to the hospital, I was familiarizing myself with my surroundings), I entered the ICU, and for some reason was drawn to the bedside of Mr. Laffernis. From the outset, following introductions, we began developing a patient/ pastor relationship that was soon to grow into a lasting and enduring friendship. During that first encounter, I was introduced not only to Lloyd, but to his pain and suffering as well. On that initial visit, he took my hand and placed it on his ribcage and asked me to pray that the pain would not linger. To this day, I can almost feel his pain as I did on that occasion when I tried to minister to him through accurate empathy, i.e., entering into his world of suffering with him.

That was the first of many visit that I would make with Lloyd, as he would be admitted as a patient for treatment many times over during the time I knew him. Not only did I have the privilege to minister to him as a patient, on several occasions Carolyn and I visited with Lloyd and his lovely wife Ann in their beautiful Bangalore home. On one occasion as their invited guests for dinner, we were treated to Lloyd's special barbecue chicken (wrapped in aluminum foil), a dinner that was absolutely delicious. He even gave Carolyn his recipe for us to enjoy later.

By way of payback—and after finding out that Lloyd had a taste for a special kind of smoked salmon—Carolyn and I found the salmon he liked during a return trip to the States, purchased it, and brought it back to India for him to enjoy.

All the while during that first visit with him in the hospital, Lloyd seemed to be in constant pain, but his pain did not keep him from going on with his life and enjoying it. He always seemed to make the most of any given situation.

The amazing thing about Lloyd is that, in my 40 years of ministry, I never saw anyone suffer as he suffered, and yet he had developed a coping mechanism that was amazing. His trust in God, I believe, was the key to his sustaining outlook on life in spite of his suffering.

As time passed, I sensed that Lloyd was nearing the end of his life, and I wanted to be sure, to the best of my knowledge, that he knew for certain that he had received the gift of eternal life. Since his native language was Malayalam, I took a fellow pastor who spoke Malayalam with me to Lloyd's home to share the gospel with him in his language. It was on that occasion that I received the confirmation I needed of his assurance of heaven.

In December of 2011, after completing our assignment with our mission board, Carolyn and I left India and returned to our home in the States for a time. Recently, however, we were invited back to India. Now serving under a three-year contract with the hospital, we have had the opportunity to renew our friendship with Lloyd's wife, Ann. Thus it is with Ann's permission that I share Lloyd's story with you, the reader, to encourage those of you who have suffered, or may be suffering, from some kind of traumatic experience—be it physical, psychological, or emotional. I say to you that there is hope beyond the pain, as witnessed in the life of Lloyd. Lloyd has left us with an excellent example of how one can deal with suffering through effective coping by relying upon his strong faith in a loving God. Thus it is my special privilege to share with you Lloyd's story.

Suffering: A Talk Given to the Divine Providence Brothers on the 10ᵗʰ of February 2007

My dear brothers, this is a talk about suffering— my suffering and suffering in general.

In November 1996, I was excited to get a job as shipping manager in a place called Hudeidah in Yemen. Frankly, until that time, I had never heard of such a place. Once in Yemen, I got quickly involved in the day-to-day work and used to go home rather late from my office. One Monday while I was busy at work in my office, I started to feel an intense pain in my right flank. I also started having a low-grade fever in the evenings. I was also losing weight very fast. I lost seven kilograms in two weeks. That was in February 1997, three months after I went to Yemen. I took a couple of painkiller Paracetamol tablets and such. The fever and pain never left, but instead started to intensify. I decided to go to the doctor. He did an ultrasound scan on me and very calmly told me that I had a massive tumor near my right kidney. He also told me that it had to be removed as quickly as possible. Yemen did not have good hospitals, and hence I decided to return to Cochin in Kerala. (I used to live in Cochin.) My first surgery was done in Cochin in February 1997. I was diagnosed as having a very rare form of cancer called adrenocortical carcinoma, which is found in only *one* of every one or two million people worldwide. This is a type of cancer that is found on the adrenal glands. The documented life expectancy of a patient who contracts this type of cancer was only five to six years.

My thought at that time was that I would surely die. I was afraid. There was so much to do, so many unfinished dreams, and I was only an average Catholic. I used to recite the rosary, and go to church if possible, all as a matter of routine. I had never read the Bible. I believe in those days, no

Catholic home had a Bible, though I did buy one after finishing my school finals. Strangely, I had bought it not because I was interested in reading or understanding the Word of God. In those days, in order to complete the entrance exams to join the Christian Medical College in Vellore, one had to answer some questions from the Bible. I bought it to prepare for the exams! Needless to say, I did not pass the exams!

My wife and daughter are much more devout than I am; they read the Bible and other religious books and spend more time in prayer than I do. In fact, without my wife's uncomplaining love and support, I would have had a very tough time indeed.

However, before my surgery, I instinctively prayed to the Lord and told Him that I was surrendering myself to Him and that I knew He would do what was best for me. After that, I was unafraid and ready for anything.

Having undergone six surgeries, it's been only six months since my first surgery. The surgeons had to leave behind some tumors since they were inoperable. One of them has grown to 16' x 17' in size, and is the biggest tumor in my stomach. However, I have survived a good ten years plus! This is my 11th year running.

During the past seven years, despite all those surgeries, I have travelled to various countries, worked in several countries abroad, built my house in Bangalore, and watched our daughter get married. All these things happened only by the grace and blessings of the Lord.

During this period, I lost my gallbladder and my right kidney. I also underwent various other procedures over the years, and even now I am under a strong medication. I have lost considerable weight and get tired quickly. Yes, I did suffer a lot. I am still suffering the rather intense pain that comes upon me like a knife being twisted inside me. I am also suffering the inability to do things that I want to do. However, despite all this, I am a happy person and have no issues with God for keeping me in this suffering state. You may ask, *Why? How?* Well, I shall come to that eventually.

In July 2002, I went to Egypt. My stay in Egypt completely changed my life. I became more involved with the fellowship of Christ and started reading the Bible. My wife and I made a lot of friends— good Christian people. Once again, I got sick with many tumors forming in my stomach. This time I was suffering with severe pain and weight loss due to the multiple tumors on either side of my stomach. Before I left for India for another surgery, these friends came over to my house to pray for me. Friends from Egypt, friends from Sudan who were refugees fleeing from the atrocities and sufferings from Darfur, friends from Holland and England, and sisters from the Missionaries of Charity in Egypt—they all used to lay their hands on my stomach, read extensively from the Bible, and loudly pray and sing to the Lord to heal me. I was very touched, and from that time I realized that I should pray by thanking Him for the favors He has given me. I also knew that I should pray for others with the same passion that I prayed for myself.

In June 2004, I returned to India. I underwent a very major and extremely dangerous surgery. Many of my daughter's friends, including Fr. Oresto, came and prayed in front of the operating theatre throughout the surgery. I was also deeply moved when Fr. Oresto and Fr. Lawrence said Mass and gave me communion in the ward, as did Fr. Harry. Thank you, Father Oresto, and thank you dear friends of the Divine Providence for ministering to me whenever I am in need in my home. After that surgery, I had a large, cross-like scar on my stomach. My doctor told me that the cross had saved my life.

I must say that whenever I suffered with pain from the tumors, I did have my doubts. I used to ask myself, *Why me? Why now? Why is God allowing this to happen?* I searched the Bible and other religious reading materials for answers concerning God's seeming disinterest in my suffering. I also wanted to know why God allowed my illness to keep recurring, and why my suffering was a continuous process.

What I learned and put together is that suffering is a tool that God uses to get our attention and to accomplish His purpose in our lives. Could God prevent all suffering? Of course, He could. But in Romans 8:28, it is written, "And we know that God causes all things to work together for good to those who love God, to those who are called according to His purpose." So even suffering is part of "all things" that God is using to accomplish His purposes, and those who trust Him will not be disappointed. Hence, even when I am in the severe pain and in doubt, I trust my Lord in the wonderful plan. The worst things are always His best things.

I also used to think just like an atheist as to how a God of love would permit sufferings in this world such as cancer, war, pain, and so on, especially when the person who is afflicted is apparently innocent or God-fearing. I then realized that our very minds are created by God and that we can only use these minds to the extent He allows. Therefore, it was absolutely ridiculous for me to use my mind to question Him and His motives. Is it not written in Genesis, "Far be it from You to do such a thing, to slay the righteous with the wicked, so that the righteous and the wicked are *treated* alike. Far be it from You! Shall not the Judge of all the earth deal justly?" (18:25). In Romans we read, "On the contrary, who are you, O man, who answers back to God? The thing molded will not say to the molder, 'Why did you make me like this,' will it?'" (9:20).

Having settled this by faith, I also realized that my suffering was nothing compared to the suffering of the One who gave up His life for our sins. In his book *How Long, O Lord?* author D. A. Carson wrote, "Frequently it is when we are crushed and devastated that the cross speaks most powerfully to us. The wounds of Christ then become Christ's credentials. The World mocks, but we are assured of God's love by Christ's wounds."[19]

It was the Apostle Peter who wrote the following:

> "For this *finds* favor, if for the sake of conscience toward God a person bears up under sorrows when suffering unjustly. For what credit is there if, when you sin and are harshly treated, you endure it with patience? But if when you do what is right and *suffer for it* you

121

patiently endure it, this *finds* favor
with God" (1 Peter 2:19–20).

I also saw that my suffering and the miracle of
my life have apparently touched many of my friends
and even others whom I do not know directly.
Many of them have called and told me how they
felt stronger in Christ after knowing about me.
Some who never believed in miracles now believe.
I have even received money and words of support
from unknown strangers who heard of my situation
from my friends. Several preachers and brothers and
sisters from various prayer groups, friends of my
daughter, and, of course, ministers from the Divine
Providence came to my home every so often to pray
for me. It was then that I saw God's real plan for me,
and I realized then that I was indeed special. I was
special indeed to be selected to undergo the trials
of suffering. I was sure that I would go to heaven
so long as I kept to the right path. I confided to
my wife that the Lord would not keep me alive all
these years without a reason. This was manifested
to me over the years, and I was happy. My pains
were a small issue once I realized the larger plan of
the Almighty.

I also realized that suffering provides
an opportunity for God's glory through our
transformation and testimony. When my dear
brother and friend Fr. Mariano asked me whether
I could give a talk to you about suffering, I
immediately said yes! At that time I did not know
what I would say to you. Last Sunday, I read this
passage from Thessalonians: "So that no one would
be disturbed by these afflictions; for you yourselves

know that we have been destined for this" (1 Thessalonians 3:3). And then, from the writings of Peter, I read, "Beloved, do not be surprised at the fiery ordeal among you, which comes upon you for your testing, as though some strange thing were happening to you" (1 Peter 4:12). Therefore, I knew that I was suffering as a testimony and as a witness. But I would never have imagined giving my witness to the world. I thank you, Fr. Mariano, for giving me this opportunity to be the first to bear witness to these fine young brothers, who are so blessed to be going forward spreading the Lord's ministry.

One can suffer in two ways: one is negative and the other positive.

In the negative process, one loses self-respect and is always complaining; he is whining and always angry, or cursing God and everybody else. Take the case of the Apostle Paul. St. Paul, as you well know, was chained daily to a Roman soldier in his own house. Imagine that! What a terrible suffering that would have been. However, he continued to rejoice in the Lord despite his suffering, and his suffering resulted in the spread of the gospel within the elite imperial Praetorian Guard. Would this have ever taken place if he had complained, sulked, and grown bitter? There is also that wonderful chapter on suffering found in the book of Hebrews.

There are two kinds of happiness. One is the human kind, which is derived from any of the details of life itself that are materialistic, worldly, and physical. The other is divine happiness, which is the inner joy provided by the Holy Spirit. I believe that human happiness is temporary and dependent. It lasts only for as long as one is happy with the thing that provides happiness and requires life to sustain it. God's happiness is independent of anything in this world. It does not depend on people, possessions, or circumstances. I am happy. I have God's happiness with me, and it is this deep belief that keeps me going every minute of the day or night.

I shall end this talk with another excerpt from the Bible. This passage is found in First Peter and reads, "Therefore, those also who suffer according to the will of God shall entrust their souls to a faithful Creator in doing what is right" (1 Peter 4:19). I have entrusted my sufferings to the Lord and am at peace. God bless you all.

GOD'S PROVISION

Dear wounded heart, be not dismayed; take encouragement if you are still struggling with emotional pain. There is a remedy for your hurts. There is an antidote. We have God's provisions.

God cares about your broken heart. The psalmist wrote, "The LORD is near to the brokenhearted and saves those who are crushed in spirit" (Psalm 34:18. According to the psalmist, "The sacrifices of God are a broken spirit; and a contrite heart, O God, You will not despise" (Psalm 51:17).

"God healed David's heart and He will also heal yours," says Basil Frasure.[20] Again in the words of the psalmist, "He heals the brokenhearted and binds up their wounds" (Psalm 147:3). Then in Hebrews, we read these words: "Jesus Christ is the same yesterday and today and forever" (Hebrews 13:8).

Jesus was sent into this world by the Father on a mission of mercy, not only to "seek and to save that which was lost" (Luke 19:10), but also to heal the brokenhearted. At the outset of Jesus' public ministry, following His temptations in the wilderness, He said, "The Spirit of the LORD is upon Me, because He anointed Me to preach the gospel to the poor. He has sent Me to proclaim release to the captives, and recovery of sight to the blind, to set free those who are oppressed, to proclaim the favorable year of the LORD" (Luke 4:18–19). Quoting from the prophet Isaiah, Jesus outlines, in a few short sentences, His public ministry.

Jesus Himself suffered all the hurts that one can suffer. Isaiah, the prophet, writes of the Suffering Servant in a passage that is often referred to as The Servant Song (Isaiah 53:1-12). Breaking in on this most beautiful passage of Scripture at verse three, we read the following:

> "He was despised and forsaken of men, a man of sorrows and acquainted with grief; And like one from whom men hide their face He was despised, and we did not esteem Him, Surely our grief He Himself bore, And our sorrows He carried; Yet we ourselves esteemed Him stricken, smitten of God, and afflicted. But He was pierced through for our transgressions, He was crushed for our iniquities; The chastisement for our well-being *fell* upon Him, And by His scourging we are healed" (Isaiah 53:3-5).

The evangelist John wrote in the prologue to his Gospel, "He came to His own, and those who were His own did not receive Him" (John 1:11). Consider also the following verses:

> "Then came the *first* day of Un-leavened Bread on which the Passover *lamb* had to be sacrificed" (Luke 22:7).
> "And the people stood by, looking on. And even the ruler were sneering at Him, saying, 'He saved

others; let Him save Himself if this is the Christ
of God, His chosen One'" (Luke 23:35).

"About the ninth hour Jesus cried out with
a loud voice, saying, 'Eli, Eli, LAMA
SABACHTHANI!' that is, 'MY GOD, MY
GOD, WHY HAVE YOU FORSAKEN
ME?'" (Matthew 27:46).

"Through the cross of Jesus, God has provided the healing for
your hurts."[21] "But He was pierced through for our transgressions"
(Isaiah 53:5). It was after the resurrection when Jesus appeared to
His disciples, that Jesus said to Thomas, who was not present at an
earlier appearing, "Reach here with your finger, and see My hands;
and reach here your hand and put it into My side; and do not be
unbelieving, but believing. Thomas answered and said to Him, 'My
Lord and My God!'"(John 20:27, 28).

As seen in the resurrected body of Jesus, scars from hurts do not
automatically disappear. Jesus took his scars to heaven with Him.
Although scars received in this life, from hurts, never just go away,
Jesus provides healing through His shed blood on the cross.

"It is God's desire to heal your hurts."[22] "Casting all your anxiety
on Him, because He cares for you" (I Peter 5:7). No one living on
this earth ever cared for you like Jesus. We can cast our cares and
hurt upon Him. He is big enough to handle them. According to
God's Word, He desires to heal us from all our hurts. His work is
healing. Our job is casting all of our anxiety on Him.

God must have control of your whole heart before He can heal
it. "You will seek *Me* and find Me when you search for Me with all
your heart" (Jeremiah 29:13). One of the hardest parts of receiving
personal healing from God, is that we fail to relinquish our control
to Him. Seeking Him with all our heart begins, I believe, at the
point of which we are willing to give Him full and immediate
control. After all, is He not in control of our circumstances?

"Behold, I stand at the door and knock; If anyone hears My voice and opens the door, I will come in to him and will dine with him, and he with Me" (Revelation 3:20). In the midst of our pain and suffering, Jesus reveals Himself to our conscience level of thinking. He stands at our hearts door, as it were, ready to heal our hurts, but we must invite Him in to take first place in our lives and be seated on the throne room of our hearts.

WHAT ARE THE STEPS OF PREPARATION?

The following steps are from Dr. Frasure's *Healing of the Wounded Heart*. The content is by this author.

The first step is to prepare oneself to give of one's heart to Jesus by letting Him become Lord (Lord = Ruler). That first step begins with *confession* and *belief.* We read "that if you confess with your mouth Jesus as Lord; and believe in your heart that God raised Him from the dead, you will be saved" (Romans 10:9). This is the starting point for everyone. While our experiences may be different, everyone must come to Him the same way. Jesus said, "I am the way, and the truth, and the life; no one come to the Father but through Me" (John 14:6).

In my estimation, Reverend Dr. Billy Graham is one of the greatest evangelists of the twentieth century. I have often heard him say the following when giving the invitation to receive the gift of eternal life: Three things are involved in coming to Christ: 1) The emotions. A person must be sorry that they have broken the heart of God. 2) The intellect. A person must realize that they are a sinner in need of being saved. 3) The will. A person must be willing to turn from sin and self and turn to Jesus.

This is repentance. In essence, then, a person must come to Jesus by faith, letting Him become the Lord (i.e., Ruler) of their life, confessing with their mouth that He is Lord, and believing in their heart that He died on the cross, was buried, arose from the dead, and ascended to heaven to purchase for them a place that He offers as a free gift. This is the first step of preparation to find healing for the soul.

I think of a sermon illustration I once heard about Abraham and the offering of his son, Isaac. As the story goes, when Abraham lifted the knife to take the life of his son, God stayed his hand. What He wanted from Abraham was not his son as a sacrifice—He wanted the heart of Isaac's father. God wants us to give Him our heart as well. Jesus made that possible through His death, burial, and glorious resurrection. Paul explains that as a result of Jesus' obedience to death on a cross, "For this reason also God highly exalted Him, and bestowed on Him the name which is above every name, so that at the name of Jesus EVERY KNEE WILL BOW, of those who are in heaven and on earth and under the earth" (Philippians 2:9-10).

The second step of preparation involves forgiveness. If you have offended someone else, then you must confess your offense and ask him or her to forgive you. The evangelist Matthew tells us how:

> "Therefore if you are presenting your offering at the altar, and there remember that your brother has something against you, leave your offering there before the altar and go; first be reconciled to your brother, and then come and present your offering" (Matthew 5:23-24).

Many years ago, prior to my surrender to full-time ministry and while I was serving as a deacon in my local church, my best friend (also a deacon in the same church) and I had a conflict over a church-related problem. Before the conflict could be resolved, it developed into a broken relationship that lasted for two years. We went our separate ways with broken spirits and wounds that reached down into our very souls. During those two years, we did not have contact with one another, and peace evaded us. In the meantime, I responded to God's call to the ministry. My friend, who was now living in another state, heard about my call and took the initiative; while he was back in town, he invited me to meet with him at a local restaurant. The two of us arrived at the restaurant at the same time. He got out of his car. I got out of mine. We embraced and forgave each other, and our relationship was no longer broken. The hurt and pain both of us suffered over that broken relationship had now begun to heal, and our friendship was renewed.

Forgiveness includes those who hurt and slander us. The words of Peter speak to this issue. He has written, "And keep a good conscience so that in the thing in which you are slandered, those who revile your good behavior in Christ will be put to shame" (I Peter 3:16).

The third step of preparation involves releasing of the person who has hurt you. The truth is revealed in what has become known as the Model Prayer. We break in on the prayer at verse 12: "And forgive us our debts, as we also have forgiven our debtors. . . . For if you forgive others their transgressions, your heavenly Father will forgive you. But if you do not forgive others, then your Father will not forgive your transgressions" (Matthew 6:12, 14–15).

During my second pastorate after graduating from seminary, I sat in my study across from a young wife and mother who had separated from her husband by divorce, and soon thereafter became involved in another relationship. Now loaded with guilt, and openly realizing that she had made a terrible mistake in divorcing the man she loved she came to me for help. During the counseling session, she took responsibility for her actions, united with the church where I served, was baptized, and then asked me for help in getting her husband back. I was quick to explain to her that this would be an uphill battle at best, especially since she was already involved in another relationship. I phoned her husband a few days later, however, and stated the reason for my call. He was, at first, a bit reluctant to make an appointment but finally agreed to meet with me. During our first meeting, I sensed that he was deeply wounded, hurt, angry, and bitter toward his wife. As I hoped would happen, after that first difficult meeting he continued to meet with me, and I dealt with his spiritual need.

Eventually, he agreed to meet with his wife in my study. To make a long story short, after several counseling sessions, he forgave his wife and asked her to remarry him. They wanted to get married right away, and I recommended that they go to the justice of the peace for a legal ceremony, after which I would do premarital counseling and give them a Christian wedding in due time. They both agreed. They were remarried as I recommended. He was baptized and became a member of the church, and soon thereafter they were pregnant with their second child.

After many years, they are still together and now have grandchildren. Thus their story of forgiveness and reconciliation is one for the record.

What happened in this case was that the wounded husband was willing to forgive his wife for the wrong she had dealt him and release her from the guilt she had been carrying. On the other hand, she was willing to take responsibility for her actions, and ask her husband to forgive her. One teaching that can be gleaned from this story is that divorce does not have to be the end. For this couple, reconciliation was a new beginning that continues to this day. In keeping with the passage above, they forgave each other, and God forgave them.

The fourth step in preparation involves yielding one's rights—including possessions, respect, family, and expectations—to God. This truth is revealed in the story of a young man who is often referred to as The Rich Young Ruler. The story unfolds like this: "And someone (Rich Young Ruler) came to Him and said, 'Teacher, what good thing shall I do that I may obtain eternal life?' And He (Jesus) said to him, 'Why are you asking me about what is good? There is *only* One who is good; but if you wish to enter into life, keep the commandments.' *Then* He said to Him, 'Which ones?' And Jesus said, 'YOU SHALL NOT COMMIT MURDER; YOU SHALL NOT COMMIT ADULTRY; YOU SHALL NOT

STEAL; YOU SHALL NOT BEAR FALSE WITNESS; HONOR YOUR FATHER AND MOTHER; and YOU SHALL LOVE YOUR NEIGHBOR AS YOURSELF.' The young man said to Him, 'All these things I have kept; What am I still lacking?' Jesus said to Him, 'If you wish to be complete, go *and* sell your possessions and give to *the* poor, and you will have treasure in heaven; and come, follow me.' But when the young man heard this statement, he went away grieving; for he was one who owned much property" (Matthew 19:16-22). The world was too much with this young man and he would live to suffer the consequences of his wrong decision. He was unwilling to yield his rights (let go of his possessions), and trust Jesus to meet his need.

"You younger men, likewise, be subject to *your* elders; and all of you, clothe yourselves with humility toward one another, for GOD OPPOSED TO THE PROUD, BUT GIVES GRACE TO THE HUMBLE. Therefore humble yourselves under the mighty hand of God, that He may exalt you at the proper time" (I Peter 5:5-6) Humility to God, and before others, positions a person who has fallen, to be lifted up in due time. Emotional pain and hurt, however, at the hands of others, if humility is not practiced (turning the other cheek as it were), can cause hardness of heart and an unforgiven spirit in the life of the one offended. "Therefore," we are admonished in Scripture to humble ourselves and let God take care of the vengeance. Submission (linking oneself under God's authority) is the ingredient to find grace that God has for the humble.

"And He summoned the crowd with His disciples, and said to them, 'If anyone wishes to come after Me, he must deny himself, and take up his cross and follow Me. For whoever wishes to save his life will lose it, but whoever loses his life for My sake and the gospel's will save it. For what does it profit a man to gain the whole world, and forfeit his soul? For what will a man give in exchange for his soul?" (Mark 8:34-37). There is a high price to be paid to gain, and maintain, worldly possessions that we cannot keep. Living in a materialistic world, this is a hard lesson to learn for many, and even harder to practice. One must hold loosely the things of this world and run hard after God for the things, which are eternal.

"Those who love Your law has great peace, and nothing causes them to stumble" (Psalm 119:165). Hiding God's Word in One's heart is the best assurance for a more stable life, great peace, and assurance against stumbling along the way.

You must put your judgment into God's hands and then ask God to forgive them for their offenses toward you. "And Pilate pronounced sentence that their demand be granted" (Luke 23:24). When others hurt us, we must let go, and let God! God will take care of the judging. Our part is the forgiving. Some Biblical examples of forgiveness...In Genesis, "Joseph forgave his brothers who sold him into slavery." When Stephen was being stoned, he said, "Lord, do not hold this sin against them!" (Acts 7:60). The greatest example in the Bible, however, is Jesus dying on the cross when He said, "Father, forgive them, for they do not know what they are doing" (Luke 23:34).

There is a warning to the steps of preparation..."A wounded heart that doesn't receive healing is an open door for evil spirits." "BE ANGRY, AND DO NOT SIN; do not let the sun go down on your anger, and do not give the devil an opportunity" (Ephesians 4:26-27). When there is a wound in the human body, if not treated properly, the wounded area of the body becomes a breeding ground for infectious diseases. Emotional wounds, likewise, if not dealt with effectively, gives place to the devil in delivering further hurt and pain to the wounded.

Does not the Bible say, "Be of sober *spirit* be on the alert. Your adversary, the devil, prowls around like a roaring lion, seeking someone to devour?" (I Peter 5:8).

As revealed earlier in Section II, Cain did not master his anger and as a result suffered the sad consequences of his actions. The good news, however, is that anger can be mastered if the proper steps are taken to resolve it. These steps come under the heading of "anger resolution." They are as follows (Frasure):

1. Grant forgiveness – Matthew 6:14; Colossians 3:13
2. Seek deliverance – Mark 16:17; James 4:7
3. Unload your cares – 1 Peter 5:7–9; Philippians 4:8; Luke 4:18
4. Create a new model – Romans 12:2; Philippians 4:8; 2 Corinthians 5:17
5. Break the generational curses – Galatians 3:13–14; Romans 6:1
6. Yield your personal rights to God – Philippians 2:7; Luke 9:23; 22:42; Exodus 4:2–4
7. Use Peace – Matthew 5:9; Romans 12:8; Hebrews 12:14
8. See from God's perspective – Job 42:5; Psalm 73:17–28

"Then Peter came and said to Him, 'Lord, how often shall my brother sin against me and I forgive him? Up to seven times? Jesus said to him, 'I do not say to you, up to seven times, but up to seventy times seven" (Matthew 18:21-22).

HOW DOES A PERSON RECEIVE HEALING?

The following steps were taken from Basil Frasure's *Healing of the Wounded Heart*.

1. Make a list of your sins: "Search me, O God, and know my heart; Try me and know my anxious thoughts; And see if there be any hurtful way in me, And lead me in the way everlasting" (Psalm 139:23-24).). Find a quiet place where you can be alone without

interruption. Take with you two or three blank sheets of paper and a pen or pencil. Then, having given the Holy Spirit permission to search you, begin writing down the sins He brings to your mind. Continue the process of listening and writing as long as God's Spirit is convicting you of sin, i.e., bringing to the surface of your conscious level of thinking sins that you have committed. Once that process is completed, get on your knees before God and spread your list of sins out in front of you. Now move to the next step . . .

2. Begin with the greatest first. Your eyes and your mind, under the guidance of God's Spirit, will direct you to the greatest first if you are sensitive to His prompting. Continue that process until you have exhausted, and dealt with, all the sins you have written down. Once that is completed, you are ready to move to the next step . . .

3. Ask God to cleanse you of all wrong attitudes (anger, bitterness, lust, unforgiveness, hate, revenge, and so on). Then focus your attention on the following verse: "Come now, and let us reason together, Says the LORD, though your sins are as scarlet, They will be white as snow; Though they are red like crimson, They will be like wool" (Isaiah 1:18). Then adapt David's prayer to your need by "praying the psalm back to God"—for example, "Create in me a clean heart, O God, And renew a steadfast spirit within me" (Psalm 51:10).

Now, having completed the above steps in order to receive healing, and having confessed all the known sins in your life, and after agreeing with Him that you have sinned, and upon meeting His conditions for healing, you can claim His promise while knowing and believing that you have been cleansed of your sins: "If we confess our sins, He is faithful and righteous to forgive us our sins and to cleanse us from all unrighteousness" (1 John 1:9).

Now that you have a clean slate, as it were, you can destroy the paper on which your sins were recorded and claim God's promise of complete forgiveness. Now move on to the next step . . .

4. Picture your experience of being hurt in your mind. Then picture Jesus suffering the same hurt for you and overcoming it by His own death and resurrection. Remember that "He Himself bore our sins in His body on the cross, so that we might die to sin and live to righteousness; for by His wounds you were healed" (I Peter 2:24).

5. In faith, ask God to heal your wounded heart in the name of Jesus. "Moreover, I will give you a new heart and put a new spirit within you; and I will remove the heart of stone from your flesh and give you a heart of flesh," we read in Ezekiel 36:26. And in John we read, "In that day you will not question Me about anything. Truly, Truly, I say to you, if you ask the Father for anything in My name, He will give it to you" (John 16:23).

Once you have been healed, you then become like Jesus—a wounded healer—and then you can begin your ministry of healing. Here is how the ministry of healing unfolds . . .

1. As God heals your hurts, He will give you a tender heart that will be sensitive to the hurts of others. We read, "Now all these things are from God, who reconciled us to Himself through Christ and gave us the ministry of reconciliation" (2 Corinthians 518); and "He said to him, 'Go home to your people and report to them what great things the Lord has done for you, and *how* He had mercy on you'" (Mark 5:19).

2. "God will change that which was meant for evil into good: "As for you, you meant evil against me, but God meant it for good in order to bring about this present result, to preserve many people alive" (Genesis 50:20).

The process of learning to forgive and forget is clearly revealed in the Old Testament story of Joseph in Genesis 37—50. In this story of Joseph, it can clearly be seen that if anyone had a right to be bitter, hurt, vengeful, and unforgiving, it was Joseph. Somewhere along the way, however, Joseph must have made things right with God. Thus, rather than harbor unforgiveness in his heart for what his brothers did to him in the past, Joseph forgave them and refused to remember the hurt he had experienced at their hands. Instead of getting even, Joseph took the opportunity to exercise forgiveness and demonstrate his character. As the story of Joseph's life unfolds, we see that by the time one comes to chapter 50, 17 years have passed, Joseph's father Israel (Jacob) has died, and Joseph's brothers are still living in fear of what Joseph might do to them. At that time, Joseph reassures them that he has truly forgiven them. This truth is revealed as follows:

> When Joseph's brothers saw that their father was dead, they said, "What if Joseph bears a grudge against us and pays us back in full for all the wrong which we did to him!" . . . But Joseph said to them, "Do not be afraid, for am I in God's place? As for you, you meant evil against me, but God meant it for good in order to bring about this present result, to preserve many people alive" (Genesis 50:15, 19–20).

As revealed in the story of Joseph, forgiveness is based on three biblical truths: 1) truth surfaces the hurt, 2) forgiveness takes the sting out of the hurt, and 3) forgiveness is based on our trust in the sovereignty of God.

And now along those same lines of thought, I share with you seven practical truths taken from a sermon series by Dr. Fred Lowery titled *Advancing Through Adversity*:

1. Forgetting begins with asking for forgiveness from those whom we have injured.
2. Forgetting means forgiving those who have injured us.
3. Forgetting will not come immediately.
4. Forgetting is a reminder to me that I, too, have flaws.

5.   Forgetting is impossible without repentance.
6.   Forgetting always requires forgiveness.
7.   Forgetting sets us free from the past, gives us peace in the present, and enables us to face the future without fear.[23]

In light of the above list, and as revealed in the life of Joseph (Genesis 37—50), forgiveness is a choice, and we can choose to forgive and forget it—forgetting not in the sense that we will no longer remember the hurt and pain we suffered from others, but in the sense that the sting of the hurt has been removed. For example, a father and son were taking a trip together in the family car when suddenly a honeybee appeared. The son began to scream and move close to his father because he was terrified of bees. The father caught the bee in his hand and squeezed it lightly. He then opened his hand, in which the bee was struggling to stay alive, and said to his son, "Now my son, you no longer have to be afraid of the bee. It cannot hurt you now! The stinger has been removed." The bee's stinger was now in the father's hand. He had removed the threat of his son being harmed by the honeybee, and the son no longer had to be afraid. That is what Jesus did for us on the cross when He said, "Father, forgive them, for they do not know what they are doing" (Luke 23:34). On the cross, Jesus not only removed the sting of death, He also enabled us to forgive those who have hurt us, thus removing the sting.

> "Nevertheless, the LORD your God was not willing to listen to Balaam, but the LORD your God turned the curse into a blessing for you because the LORD your God loves you" (Deuteronomy 23:5).
> "And we know that God causes all things to work together for good to those who love God, to those who are called according to *His* purpose" (Romans 8:28).

137

"But if we are afflicted, it is for your comfort
and salvation; or if we are comforted, it's for
your comfort, which is effective in the patient
enduring of the same suffering which we also
suffer" (II Corinthians 1:6).

3. Ask God to fill you with His Spirit, His love, and His grace, that
you may share the healing that you have received with others, that
they may be healed.

"So that Christ may dwell in your hearts
through faith; *and* that you, being rooted and
grounded in love, may be able to comprehend with
all the saints what is the breath and length and
height and depth, and to know the love of Christ
which surpasses knowledge, that you may be filled
up to the fullness of God" (Ephesians 3:17-20).

"Therefore let us draw near with confidence to
the throne of grace, so that we may receive
mercy and find grace to help in time of need"
(Hebrews 4:16).

"Now on the last day, the great day of the feast,
Jesus stood and cried out, saying, 'If anyone
is thirsty, let him come to Me and drink. He
who believes in Me, as the Scripture said, From
his innermost being will flow rivers of living
water'" (John 7:37, 38).

4. Claim for yourself the following passage:

"THE SPIRIT OF THE LORD IS UPON
ME, BECAUSE HE ANOINTED ME TO
PREACH THE GOSPEL TO THE POOR. HE

HAS SENT ME TO PROCLAIM RELEASE TO THE CAPTIVES, AND RECOVERY OF SIGHT TO THE BLIND, TO SET FREE THOSE WHO ARE OPPRESSED, TO PROCLAIM THE FAVORABLE YEAR OF THE LORD" (Luke 4:18-19).

5. Share in the light that which you have learned in the dark. "Heal the sick, raise *the* dead, cleanse *the* lepers, cast out demons. Freely you receive, freely give" (Matthew 10:8).

CONCLUSION

The writing of this book, like my 40 plus years as a pastor, missionary and chaplain, for both Carolyn and I, our ministry has been, and is, an adventure in progress. Like the conclusion of this book, it was not until the last few months at our Northwest church, that the conflict began and eventually escalated into a major church battle. Prior to the conflict, however, a pastor could not have enjoyed a more prosperous and successful tenure as pastor. Therefore, in my concluding remarks, I will attempt to show the developmental stages of the conflict from beginning to the end, in prayerful anticipation, that you, the reader, will be blessed and that God will be glorified. First, we will consider...

THE SITUATION

After I tried several different approaches to conflict resolution, the situation went from bad to worse. It was during the interim between conflict resolution and my desire to resign that my trusted friend sent me a book in the mail on the subject of termination (afore mentioned).

At the time, both my wife and I were surprised that our mutual friend had sent us a book dealing with termination. Little did we know, however, that this book would be a source of strength and encouragement as we ultimately faced the reality of resignation.

THE CRISIS

In retrospect of my resignation, I cannot begin to describe the minutes, weeks, and months of emotional pain that my wife, Carolyn, and I went through during the church conflict and leading up to the time when I actually resigned. The best term that I can use to describe the crisis we were in (having ministered to many bereaved families over the years) is "anticipatory grief." My anticipatory grief process included anger, fear of failure and of an uncertain future, rejection, doubt, questioning, and all the other human emotions accompanying a terminal illness. These emotional feelings resulted in mild to severe depression and the inability to make rational and sound judgment calls during the course of any day.

At 52 years of age and a long way from retirement, I remembered the professor's words, which rang loud and clear in my mind: "Men, don't resign until you have a place to go!" In the meantime, the conflict had escalated into a full-blown crisis situation for both my wife and me.

The words of the psalmist describe where I was emotionally at that time . . .

> "My heart is in anguish within me, and the terrors of death have fallen upon me. Fear and trembling come upon me; and horror has overwhelmed me. 'I said, 'Oh, that I had wings like a dove! I would fly away and be at rest. Behold, I would wander far away, I would lodge in the wilderness. I would hasten to my place of refuge from the stormy wind and tempest'" (Psalm 55:4-8).

I, like David, just wanted to escape from it all even though I did not have a place to go.

As the church conflict escalated, I tried on two different occasions to resign, but could never get a peace in my heart about it.

In my depressed and confused state of mind, I could not understand why God would not allow me to get out of the situation in which I found myself.

Like the disciples in the storm at sea about whom I have written, I cried out, "Teacher, do you not care that we (I) am perishing?" (Mark 4:38 NASB). I was crying out to the Lord for help, but it seemed at that time that He was not listening. At that point in the conflict, resignation would have been the easiest course of action I could have taken. With all my heart, I wanted to do what was best for the church and it seemed to me that the best course of action would be to resign. It was not until some weeks later, following a full-blown battle at the church on Sunday morning that spilled over into the evening service, that I came to the realization that drastic action must be taken on my part. If resignation was my lot, then so be it.

That same night, following the Sunday morning conflict, I went through a struggle of the soul. Without a doubt, it was the darkest experience of my life. The next morning, however, my answer came while going for an early morning drive through the hills near our home.

While driving and praying, I reached the very same place where I had cried out to God for help two weeks earlier, and my answer came. It was at that time and place that He spoke to my wounded heart and gave me freedom to resign with the assurance that He did care.

THE CALM

Once I had made the decision to resign, I experienced the calm after the storm. The peace of God filled my heart and soul. It was a peace that I had not experienced in long time. My healing process began on March 31, 1997—Easter Sunday—the day I resigned my pastorate. The aftermath of the storm afforded us a calm that we continue to enjoy to this day.

THE CALL

In retrospect of my call to the Northwest church to be their pastor, I have never had any doubts that I heard God's distinct call. What I realize now, however, is that I had unrealistic expectations of the church and was greatly disappointed as a result. I often go back in my mind to recall the events that led up to the call to pastor the church. From the initial interview with the search committee, to the receiving of the plane tickets, to the invitation to deliver a trial sermon, and ultimately to the call to be the pastor, excitement filled our hearts all the way.

The church responded to my leadership in a positive way up until the last one and one-half years of our five-year tenure. Even then only a small percentage of the church's membership began to make things difficult for us. During the last six months, things began to go south as the initial excitement began to decrease rapidly. It was at that point I began to experience fear and the anticipated pain of separation.

Because of the various negative experiences of those days, our hearts were wounded, as were the hearts of the people in the Midwest, whom we grew to love during our tenure with them as pastor many years earlier. Both my wife and I left the people we loved with wounded hearts, as has happened to countless congregations and pastors, to whom this book is targeted.

Hopefully, by now, you the reader have discovered what this book is about—My Wounded Heart and how we survived the storm, and how you can as well. Having suffered the pain of forced termination as a Southern Baptist pastor, I now consider myself a wounded healer. Over the years, I have witnessed countless persons suffering from deep-rooted emotional, psychological, and spiritual wounds due to firing and forced termination.

On the day of our resignation, I wrote with finality in my prayer journal, "Thank You, Father. Following the worst storm of our lives,

You, God, have brought good news!" Even though we were facing an uncertain future, we were trusting fully in the Father.

Therefore, my goal for this book, as a pastor with a hands-on ministry, has been to offer practical, biblically based counsel to the whole person (body, soul, and spirit) who has been wounded emotionally, physically, psychologically, or spiritually, and to aid them on their road to recovery.

Having received healing for my wounded heart, I have adopted the following prayer of the psalmist as my personal prayer of praise and thanksgiving to God, my heavenly Father, for His healing hand upon my life and restored ministry . . .

> "I will extol You, O LORD, for
> You have lifted me up,
> And have not let my enemies
> rejoice over me.
> O LORD my God,
> I cried to You for help, and You
> healed me.
> O LORD, You have brought up
> my soul from Sheol;
> You have kept me alive, that I
> would not go down to the pit...
> Weeping may last for the night,
> But a shout of joy comes in the
> morning" (Psalm 30:1-3, 5b).

EPILOGUE

Storms come and storms go.

This is true of life storms as well. They come and they go, but often do a lot of damage to human emotions before dissipating. It is during the healing and recovery period, following the storms of life that persons react and/or respond in various ways.

While in the storm, survival becomes the major concern and reaction, rather than response, becomes the order of the moment. Once the storm is over, however, one has time to respond to the situation, reflect on past traumatic events, deal with the trauma to which one has been subjected, and ultimately find healing and full recovery if all the coping mechanisms are in place.

After the storm was over, we found ourselves in its wake and began to discover healing and restoration. Healing did not come immediately, nor did full recovery. Over a period of time, however, through forgiving and forgetting (though not in the sense of not remembering), the sting of the hurt was removed, and this was followed by full recovery. We got our lives back, as it were, and the joy of living and serving was restored.

APPENDIX

It was out of the call, followed by the crisis, and ultimately the calm that the Wounded Heart Ministries, Inc. (based on Psalm 109:22) was born. Our call to establish a wounded heart ministry took place on October 20, 1999, while at a mountain retreat in the Great Smoky Mountains of East Tennessee. Prior to our call to begin such a work of ministry, Carolyn and I had ministered to hurting pastors and families for many years, but had never had a name for our ministry until we were wounded ourselves and in need of healing.

Since that "mountaintop experience," the Wounded Heart Ministry, Inc., has been chartered and incorporated, and has received tax exemption status as a non-profit organization under the Internal Revenue Code 501(c)(3). We are up and running on the Internet at www.woundedheart.org.

In retrospect of traversing through trials ourselves, I realize a ministry was established through the ultimate recovery from crisis and emotional wounds, and not without emotional scars. Now fully recovered from our emotional wounds, we have been led by the Great Physician down paths to new adventures of ministry and service.

Why did I choose to write this book? I chose to write this book for the wounded—to show that there is peace beyond the pain. I will also soon show why this book and Wounded Heart Ministry are so needed according to statistics. But first, I share with you, the reader, the portion of a letter I received from a fellow minister who shares the same concerns that we do at the Wounded Heart Ministry. He writes . . .

> You may be aware that around one thousand Southern Baptist pastors are fired each and every year. That number does not include those pressured out, short of being fired. It also does not include those who resign because they are burned out or disillusioned. Neither does it include an associate pastor who might fit into any of these three categories, nor the huge number of pastors who remain in their churches but are weary and struggle every day. Add all these together, along with their families, and it is a staggering number of wounded servants. At the same time, these painful experiences do not happen in a vacuum. Many churches and church members are deeply wounded in these experiences. A lot of churches never recover an effective ministry, and many a member drops out, never to return.

Now I share with you some statistics that were reported on The 700 Club on October 9, 2001:

- 30 percent of pastors are fired each year.
- 50 percent feel unable to meet the needs of the job.
- 80 percent believe that pastoral ministry has affected their family in a negative way.
- 33 percent say that being in the ministry is a hazard to their family.
- 70 percent say they have lower self-esteem than when they started out in the ministry.

- 40 percent report a serious conflict with parishioners at least once a month.
- 70 percent do not have someone they consider a close friend.

Statistics also testify that fifteen hundred pastors per month drop out of the ministry. In the Southern Baptist Convention, this means that six thousand drop out and twelve hundred are fired each year.

In churches where the pastor is fired, termination is brought about by no more than 10 percent of the congregation. This means that 90 percent of the congregation sits silently by and does nothing to stop it. The 700 Club suggested that maybe those 10 percent should be put out of the church instead of the pastor.

The good news for persons in ministry, nevertheless, is that not only does God reveal the need when He calls a person to a particular ministry; He gives them the resources to meet the need. The psalmist gives witness to that fact when he writes, "With my mouth I will give thanks abundantly to the LORD; and in the midst of many I will praise Him. For He stands at the right hand of the needy, to save him from those who judge his soul" (Psalm 109:30, 31). Furthermore, according to God's Word, the Lord not only "stands at the right hand of the needy," He also "holds His pastors in His right hand" (Revelation 1:20).

By way of witnessing to the presence of God during difficult times, I have written in the margin of my Bible these words: "During my difficult church ordeal, He stood at the right hand of this needy one." Therefore, to the reader of this book I say that He will do the same for you. One of the goals of the Wounded Heart Ministry, along with this book, is to stand alongside God's wounded servants during their time of need and to assure them that He stands at the right hand of the needy to rescue, release, and restore.

Therefore, wounded servant, take courage and be encouraged. There is peace beyond the pain.

NOTES

Section I

1   Willy Nelson, *On The Road Again,* (Nashville, Tennessee On The Road Again by Willy Nelson, 1980).

2   Steve Green, *Children Are A Treasure of The Lord,* (Steve Green Ministries).

3   Charles Stanley, *How to Handle Adversity,* (Thomas Nelson Publisher, Nashville, Tennessee, 1989), Page 22.

4   Ibid., 173.

5   Martin Luther, *A Mighty Fortress Is Our God,* (Convention Press, Nashville, Tennessee), Page 40.

6   *I know not what the future holds, but I know who holds the future, -Author Unknown*

7   Charles Stanley, *Advancing Through Adversity,* (Thomas Nelson Publishers, Nashville, Atlanta, London, Vancouver, 1996), Page 94.

8   Ibid., 85.

9   Myra Marshall, with Dan McGee, Ph.D., and Jennifer Bryon Owen, *Beyond Termination: A Spouse's Story of Pain and Healing,* (Broadman Press, Nashville, 1990).

10   W. Phillip Keller, *Thank You Father: Reflections on His Walk With God,* (Word Publishing, Dallas-London-Vancouver-Melbourne, 1990), Page 72.

Section II

1   Charles Stanley, *In Touch Ministry,* (First Baptist Church, Atlanta, Georgia), (quote from a sermon on television).),

2   Basil Frasure, Ph.D., *My Wounded Heart,* (Basil Frasure, San Angelo, Texas), Website: Whole Person Counseling, wpcouse@wcc.net).

3   Ibid.

4   Ibid.

5   Vance Havner, *Fourscore: Living Beyond The Promise*, (Fleming H. Revelle Company, Old Tappan, New Jersey, 1982), Page 107.

6   D. James Kennedy, *Training Notebook-Level I*, (Evangelism Explosion International, Fort Lauderdale, Florida, 2004).

7   Basil Frasure, Ph.D., *My Wounded Heart*, (Whole Person Counseling, San Angelo, Texas), Website: wpcouse@wcc.net.

8   W. Phillip Keller, *Thank You Father: Reflections on His Walk With God*, (Word Publishing, Dallas-London-Vancouver-Melbourne, 1990), Page 11.

9   Basil Frasure, Ph.D., *My Wounded Heart*, (Whole Person Counseling, San Angelo, Texas), Website: wpcouse@wcc.net.

10 Ibid.

11 W. Phillip Keller, *Thank You Father: Reflects on His Walk With God*, (Word Publishing, Dallas-London-Vancouver-Melbourne, 1990), Page 72.

12 Basil Frasure, Ph.D., *My Wounded Heart*, (Whole Person Counseling, San Angelo, Texas), Website: wpcouse@wcc.net.

13 Ibid.

14 Ibid.

15 Henry T. Blackaby and Claude King, *Experiencing God*, (B & H Publishing Group, Nashville, Tennessee, 1998).

16 16. Katherine Marshall, *To Live Again*, (Baker Publishing Group, (Bloomington Minnesota, 1984).

17 Basil Frasure, Ph.D., *My Wounded Heart*, (Whole Person Counseling, San Angelo, Texas), Website: (wpcouse@wcc.net).

18 Scott Floyd, *Crisis Counseling: A Guide for Pastors and Professionals*, Kregel Academic & Professional, 2008), Page 100.

19 D. A. Carson, *How Long, O Lord? Reflections On Suffering and Evil*, (Baker Academic: A Division of Baker Publishing Group, Grand Rapids, Michigan, 1990, 2006). (Grand Rapids, MI:

20 Basil Frasure Ph.D., *My Wounded Heart*, (Whole Person Counseling, San Angelo, Texas), Website: (wpcouse@wcc.net).

21 Ibid.

22 Ibid.

23 Fred Lowrey, *Advancing Through Adversity*, (The First Word, Bossier City, Louisiana, 2013). (Sermons under the title: The First

Made in the USA
Columbia, SC
03 July 2017